FREE
(AND ALMOST FREE)
THINGS FOR TEACHERS

FREE
(AND ALMOST FREE)
THINGS FOR TEACHERS

Susan Osborn

A Perigee Book

Perigee Books
are published by
The Putnam Publishing Group
200 Madison Avenue
New York, NY 10016

Library of Congress Cataloging-in-Publication Data

Osborn, Susan.
   Free (and almost free) things for teachers / Susan Osborn.
      p.   cm.
   Rev. ed. of: Free things for teachers. 1987.
   ISBN 0-399-51635-2
   1. Teaching—Aids and devices—Catalogs.   2. Free material—
Catalogs.   I. Osborn, Susan.   Free things for teachers.
II. Title.
LB1043.Z907   1990   90-36840   CIP
016.37213′078—dc20

Printed in the United States of America

1   2   3   4   5   6   7   8   9   10

CONTENTS

All of the items listed in this volume
were available at press time. While we
and the suppliers have every hope that
the items will be available through
1990, we cannot guarantee this.

I. Introduction

Free Things for Teachers is one of the most valuable teaching resources you will ever own. Use it to fill your classroom with materials that will fascinate and motivate your students, and make your job easier. No item listed costs more than $5.00, and most are absolutely free!

Enriching your classroom and curriculum need not be expensive. Publishers, manufacturers, government agencies, and others offer booklets, posters, maps, worksheets, records, videos, learning kits, lesson plans, teaching guides—and much more—just for the asking! You can receive reprints from "The Curious Naturalist" from the Massachusetts Audubon Society, a study in shoemaking from the Brown Shoe Company, membership in the Benjamin Franklin Stamp Club from the Post Office,

rhythm instruments from The Children's Book & Music Center, and hundreds of other useful and creative teaching aids.

Free Things for Teachers is primarily geared for the elementary school teacher, but we're sure that every teacher will find it a worthwhile source of information and ideas.

The authors have made sure that *Free Things for Teachers* is clear, practical, and easy to use. You will find extensive listings, complete ordering information, full descriptions of all materials, and helpful tips on how to use them.

Now you have the book that lets you bring the world into your classroom at the lowest possible cost. Enjoy using it, and have fun making your classroom brighter and more exciting than ever.

II. Animals and Pets

Kids and Cats

How many cats do you know? Do you know one with tiger stripes? And one with spots? And one with seven toes? Every cat is a little bit different from every other cat, but each one wants a kind owner.

The Animal Welfare Institute's illustrated, easy-to-read booklet tells children how to be good cat owners and what to do if your cat climbs up a tree. Single copies free.

Send: request on school letterhead

Ask for: "Kittens and Cats"

Write to: Animal Welfare Institute
P.O. Box 3650
Washington, DC 20007

Befriending Animals

"Befriending Animals" is a reprint of an article from *Childhood Education*, which is designed to help primary teachers instill their students with positive attitudes toward animals. This article includes information on both wild animals and pets, and discusses the need for understanding and communication.

Send: a postcard

Ask for: "Befriending Animals"

Write to: Animal Welfare Institute
P.O. Box 3650
Washington, D.C. 20007

Meet the Animals

Here is the ideal wall chart for very young schoolchildren. "13 Pet and Farm Animals" is filled with delightful full-color illustrations of all sorts of animals: cows, parrots, mice, ducks, and more! A wonderful way for children to become familiar with different types of animals and test their identification skills. And at $24\frac{1}{2}'' \times 15\frac{3}{4}''$, this wall chart is a perfect decorative piece as well.

Send: $1.95 (plus $2.50 postage & handling)

Ask for: 3169 0 "13 Pet and Farm Animals" No. 559

Write to: Ladybird Books, Inc.
P.O. Box 1690
Auburn, ME 04211-9970

The Animal Connection

Having a guinea pig or a hamster to take care of can be a fun and valuable way of teaching students about the responsibilities and rewards of owning pets. As children care for their animals and watch them grow, they too experience the magic of growth and change, learning to respect the animals around them. Caring for a classroom pet is just one of many ways to teach kids to respect the animal kingdom. The MSPCA publishes this innovative teacher's booklet of classroom activities and discussions designed to foster humane attitudes among kids.

Send: $1.00

Ask for: "The Animal Connection"

Write to: MSPCA Humane Education Division
Circulation Dept.
350 S. Huntington Ave.
Boston, MA 02130

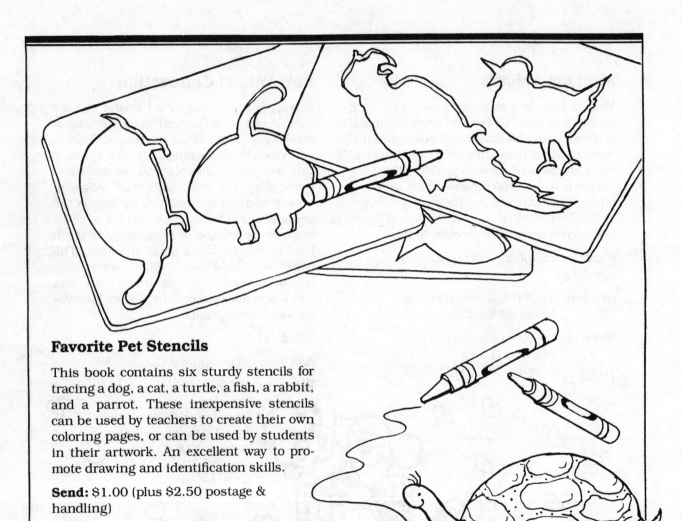

Favorite Pet Stencils

This book contains six sturdy stencils for tracing a dog, a cat, a turtle, a fish, a rabbit, and a parrot. These inexpensive stencils can be used by teachers to create their own coloring pages, or can be used by students in their artwork. An excellent way to promote drawing and identification skills.

Send: $1.00 (plus $2.50 postage & handling)

Ask for: "Fun With Favorite Pets Stencils"

Write to: Dover Publications, Inc.
31 East 2nd Street
Mineola, NY 11501

Kids and Their Canine Friends

If a child reads the Animal Welfare Institute's booklet on dogs and their masters, he or she will learn that dogs prefer good manners, need to eat and play, and require a shelter and regular doses of human kindness. Delightfully illustrated and easy to read. Single copies free.

Send: request on school letterhead

Ask for: "You and Your Dog"

Write to: Animal Welfare Institute
P.O. Box 3650
Washington, DC 20007

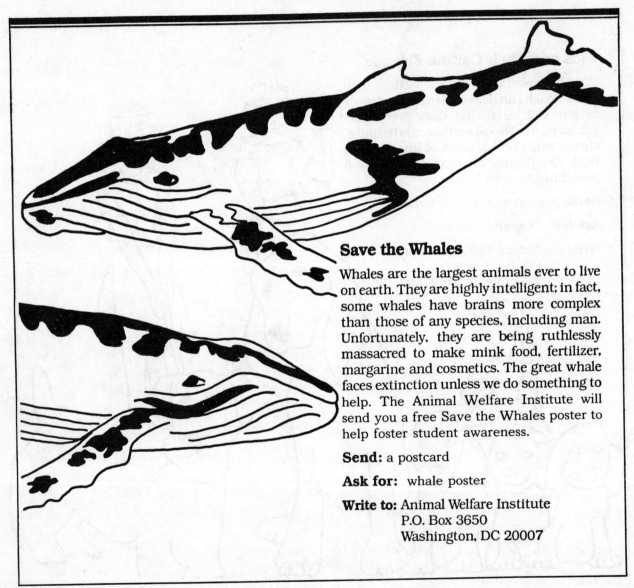

Save the Whales

Whales are the largest animals ever to live on earth. They are highly intelligent; in fact, some whales have brains more complex than those of any species, including man. Unfortunately, they are being ruthlessly massacred to make mink food, fertilizer, margarine and cosmetics. The great whale faces extinction unless we do something to help. The Animal Welfare Institute will send you a free Save the Whales poster to help foster student awareness.

Send: a postcard

Ask for: whale poster

Write to: Animal Welfare Institute
P.O. Box 3650
Washington, DC 20007

Living with Animals

The citizens of Critterton guide Carla and Michael Foster through their town as they examine the roles of animals and "animal people." The children learn much about the basic interdependency of animals and people and the cooperative nature of community living. A 23"-by-29" coloring poster ties the chapters together and illustrates the "complete" nature of the community. Suitable for intermediate readers.

Send: $1.50

Ask for: "Living with Animals" book and poster

Write to: MSPCA Humane Education
Division
Circulation Dept.
350 S. Huntington Ave.
Boston, MA 02130

III. Arts and Crafts

Mythical Beasts Coloring Book

A noted designer and former editor of *American Artist* has created 30 attractive drawings of fabled creatures for this coloring book. Old favorites such as the mermaid, the centaur, and the phoenix are here, as well as the lesser-known basilisk, kraken, and manticore. Informative captions accompany each drawing.

Send: $2.50 (plus $2.50 postage & handling)

Ask for: "Mythical Beasts Coloring Book"

Write to: Dover Publications, Inc.
31 E. 2nd St.
Mineola, NY 11501

Fridolf Johnson

MYTHICAL BEASTS
COLORING BOOK

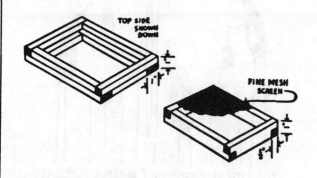

Making Paper by Hand

People have been making paper by hand for over 1,500 years, and now you and your students can too. Hammermill Papers will provide you with a packet that contains a booklet giving full illustrated instructions for the making of paper by hand. With the exception of the deckle and mold (a simple woodworking project), all the equipment necessary can be found in the home economics room.

Send: 25¢

Ask for: "How to Make Paper by Hand"

Write to: Hammermill Papers Group
6400 Poplar Ave.
Memphis, TN 38197-7000

Learning Art the Natural Way

Nature's own materials can often be the most instructive tools for introducing the basics in art. Geared for younger kids, this thoughtful book places emphasis on the utilization of mud, sand, and water for down-to-earth projects.

Send: $3.00

Ask for: "Mud, Sand, and Water"
(NAEYC No. 308)

Write to: The National Association for the
Education of Young Children
1834 Connecticut Ave., N.W.
Washington, D.C. 20009-5786

Kate Greenaway's Mother Goose Coloring Book

Your kids will love coloring Little Jack Horner, Jack and Jill, and 35 other Mother Goose personalities in this 48-page book. It is full of Kate Greenaway's inimitable illustrations, which have been rendered even more colorable by Nancy Perkins.

Send: $2.50 each (plus $2.50 postage & handling)

Ask for: "Kate Greenaway's Mother Goose Coloring Book"

Write to: Dover Publications, Inc.
31 East 2nd Street
Mineola, NY 11501

From Butterflies to Dinosaurs

Coloring is not only fun and absorbing, it's also a great way to learn. In these books, children learn about "Birds from Around the World," "Butterflies," "Flowers," and "Dinosaurs." Beautiful pictures to color are accompanied by a simple informative text and a small full-color picture on each page to use as a guide.

Send: $1.95 each (plus $2.50 postage & handling)

Ask for: Coloring Book by name

Write to: Ladybird Books, Inc.
P.O. Box 1690
Auburn, ME 04211-9970

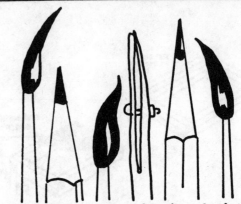

The Importance of Being Artistic in School

The Council for Basic Education, an organization whose primary purpose is the strengthening of teaching and learning in America, believes that the arts have a generative power, and in 1975, they added it to their canon of basic subjects. In this 32-page booklet, Dr. Jacques Barzun, professor emeritus at Columbia University, and Dr. Robert Saunders, art consultant in the Connecticut State Department of Education, explain just how and where the arts fit into a basic curriculum.

Send: $2.00 (plus $2.50 postage & handling)

Ask for: "Art in Basic Education"

Write to: Council for Basic Education
725 15th St., N.W.
Washington, DC 20005

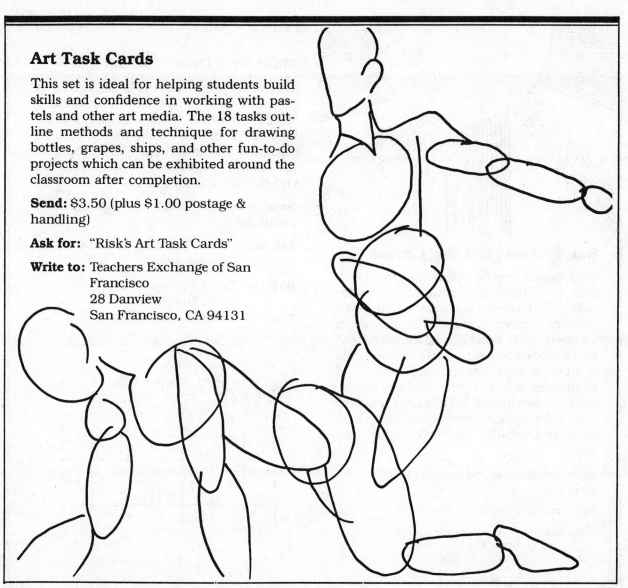

Art Task Cards

This set is ideal for helping students build skills and confidence in working with pastels and other art media. The 18 tasks outline methods and technique for drawing bottles, grapes, ships, and other fun-to-do projects which can be exhibited around the classroom after completion.

Send: $3.50 (plus $1.00 postage & handling)

Ask for: "Risk's Art Task Cards"

Write to: Teachers Exchange of San
Francisco
28 Danview
San Francisco, CA 94131

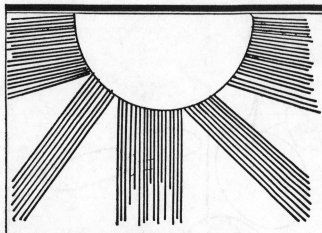

Sun-Powered Hot Dog Cooker

This experiment is meant to give you a glimpse of the future. It's a simple device that puts the sun's rays to work. With just a piece of lumber, a sheet of aluminum, a couple of nails, a pad of steel wool, a tube of household cement, a piece of aluminum foil, a ruler, a coat hanger, and a piece of sandpaper, you and your students can be the first ones in your town to have your very own solar-powered wienie roaster. Complete and detailed instructions are provided.

Send: 25¢ and a self-addressed, stamped envelope

Ask for: Solar Cooker Kit Directions

Write to: Energy Management Center
P.O. Box 190
Port Richey, FL 34673

Make Your Own Calendar

This imaginative coloring book is not only fun, but a sure-fire way to give your students a better understanding of numbers, days of the week, months, dates, seasons, and the concept of time. Because the calendar pages are blank, the book is a current calendar for any year.

Send: $2.50 (plus $2.50 postage & handling)

Ask for: "Make Your Own Calendar Coloring Book"

Write to: Dover Publications
31 E. 2nd St.
Mineola, NY 11501

Simple Woodworking

"Look, Mom, I made it myself!" Every child loves to say those words. Woodworking is a wonderful hobby because it allows children to make something that's really substantial and impressive. "Easy-to-Make Wooden Candlesticks, Chandeliers and Lamps" is filled with exact measured drawings and precise instructions for making 14 traditional projects that children will be proud to bring home.

Send: $1.75 (plus $2.50 postage & handling)

Ask for: "Easy-to-Make Wooden Candlesticks, Chandeliers and Lamps"

Write to: Dover Publications, Inc.
31 East 2nd Street
Mineola, NY 11501

Color Benjamin Bunny

One morning a little rabbit sat on a bank. He pricked his ears and listened to the trit-trot, trit-trot of a pony. A gig was coming along the road; it was driven by Mr. McGregor, and beside him sat Mrs. McGregor in her best bonnet.

This charming coloring book includes the complete unabridged text from Beatrix Potter's original 1904 edition. The 29 black-and-white illustrations allow children to share in the fun of creating some of their favorite characters.

Send: $2.00 (plus 85¢ postage & handling)

Ask for: "The Tale of Benjamin Bunny Coloring Book"

Write to: Dover Publications, Inc.
31 E. 2nd St.
Mineola, NY 11501

Patchwork Playthings

Sewing is obviously a useful skill to know, but for children it can be more than a chore. Given the right choice of project, sewing can be fun! With this book, you can help children make all sorts of toys and learn how to sew at the same time. Projects such as Humpty Dumpty, patchwork balls, or Christmas items become literally child's play with this extensively illustrated, handy guide.

Send: $2.50 (plus $2.50 postage & handling)

Ask for: "Patchwork Playthings"

Write to: Dover Publications, Inc.
31 East 2nd Street
Mineola, NY 11501

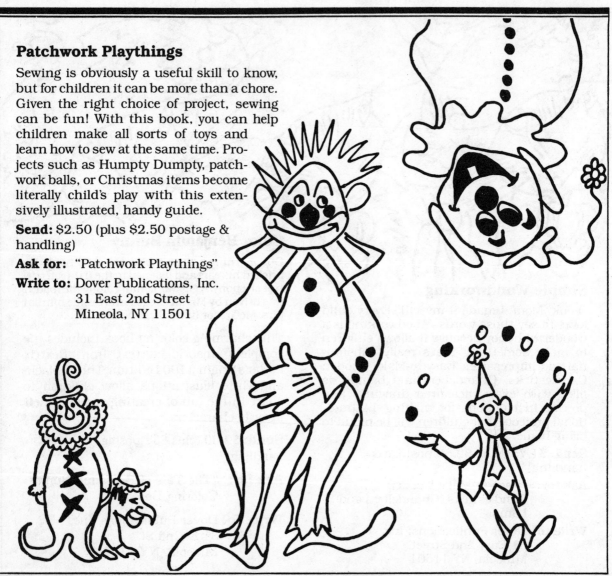

IV. Environment and Conservation

A Child's Garden

This two-color booklet lists a bounty of ideas for planting projects both in the classroom and out. Plants not only beautify the environment but also help develop a child's sense of ownership and pride. Turn your classroom into a green world and watch your students see, feel, and "grow" together. Limit one per teacher.

Send: a postcard

Ask for: "A Child's Garden"

Write to: Chevron Chemical Co.
742 Bancroft Way
Berkeley, CA 94710

Liven Up Your Classroom with a Pod of Whales

Tamar Griggs believes that science is not learned just by memory and experimentation, but also by touching the imagination and feelings of the child. She has developed a graphic way of learning about whales and conservation, and the aims of her workshop and suggested method of implementation are detailed in a flier offered by the Animal Welfare Institute. Single copies free.

Send: a self-addressed, stamped envelope

Ask for: "How to Liven Up Your Classroom with a Pod of Whales"

Write to: Animal Welfare Institute
P.O. Box 3650
Washington, DC 20007

Sierraecology Newsletter

In its ongoing efforts to bring issues of environmental concern to the public, the Sierra Club publishes a monthly newsletter designed specifically for grade school students. "Sierraecology" articles discuss current environmental threats and alternate energy sources and suggest inexpensive conservation-related activities for the classroom. School workshops and local cleanup efforts are advertised regularly, offering students an opportunity to actively join in the fight against environmental pollution.

Send: a postcard

Ask for: "Sierraecology"

Write to: Sierraecology
Sierra Club Public Affairs
730 Polk St.
San Francisco, CA 94109

Learning About Renewable Energy

The earth's supply of natural resources such as coal and oil are well on their way to becoming exhausted. Now more than ever, it has become vitally important to find ecologically sound energy alternatives. Written especially for the younger audience, this educational pamphlet introduces children to alternate energy sources, such as wind, water, and solar power, emphasizing their importance to all of our futures.

Send: a postcard

Ask for: "Learning About Renewable Energy"

Write to: Renewable Energy Information
P.O. Box 8900
Silver Spring, MD 20907

Land Reclamation

The American Coal Foundations offers a 15-page illustrated booklet which discusses many aspects of land reclamation from the land reclamation process in general to specific reclamation methods. This booklet is suitable for grades 4–12 and would fit into any section on conservation or energy.

Send: request on school letterhead

Ask for: "What Everyone Should Know About Land Reclamation"

Write to: American Coal Foundation
1130 Seventeenth Street, N.W.
Suite 220
Washington, D.C. 20036

--tap the energy that lies in our coal reserves and maintain our way of life.

--protect the balance, beauty and usefulness of our environment.

Color a Clean Environment

This coloring book is a fun and inexpensive tool for instilling environmental awareness in kids. Finished pictures can be displayed as a bright, personalized reminder of ways students can help keep their school, home, and neighborhood beautiful for everyone.

Send: 65¢.

Ask for: "Coloring Book"

Write to: Keep America Beautiful, Inc.
Communications Dept.
9 W. Broad St.
Stamford, CT 06902

Solar Reading List for Kids

The Conservation and Renewable Energy Inquiry and Referral Service has compiled a list of books about the sun and energy all of which are suitable for young readers, ages five through 12. The bibliography includes the title of the book, a summary, page length, and publisher. Help your students learn how the sun and earth can work together.

Send: a postcard

Ask for: "Solar Bibliography for Children"

Write to: Conservation and Renewable
Energy Inquiry and
Referral Service
P.O. Box 8900
Silver Spring, MD 20850

Saving by Recycling

Recycling is vital if the Earth is to survive. Research indicates that the actual practice of recycling changes attitudes—just studying it is not enough. Once people start recycling they get hooked and influence those around them. Find out what you can do to help the recycling movement. The National Recycling Coalition has free fact sheets about various aspects of recycling which can help you find out what you need to know to get your students recycling too!

Send: a self-addressed, stamped envelope

Ask for: Recycling Fact Sheets

Write to: National Recycling Coalition
1103 30th Street, NW
Suite 305
Washington, DC 20007

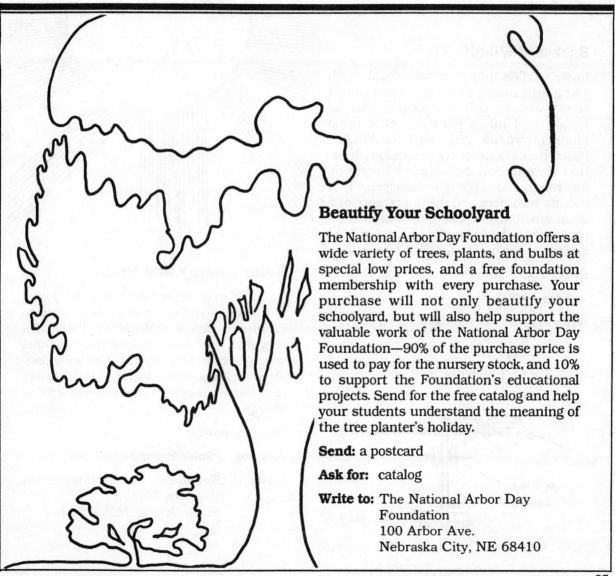

Beautify Your Schoolyard

The National Arbor Day Foundation offers a wide variety of trees, plants, and bulbs at special low prices, and a free foundation membership with every purchase. Your purchase will not only beautify your schoolyard, but will also help support the valuable work of the National Arbor Day Foundation—90% of the purchase price is used to pay for the nursery stock, and 10% to support the Foundation's educational projects. Send for the free catalog and help your students understand the meaning of the tree planter's holiday.

Send: a postcard

Ask for: catalog

Write to: The National Arbor Day
Foundation
100 Arbor Ave.
Nebraska City, NE 68410

Backyard Wildlife Kit

Invite wildlife into your schoolyard! With just a little money and a bit of planning a schoolyard or child's backyard can be transformed into a place attractive to all kinds of wildlife. The National Wildlife Federation, a nonprofit conservation education organization dedicated to informing Americans about the wise management of natural resources and the importance of a clean environment, offers an information packet that shows how to make your land an official backyard wildlife habitat.

Send: a post card

Ask for: #79301

Write to: National Wildlife Federation
Dept. 916
1412 16th St., N.W.
Washington, DC 20036

Solar Energy and You

Children everywhere have felt the power of the sun warming their faces or tried to capture its rays in their hands. "Solar Energy and You" is an informative fact sheet which describes for students how solar panels are used to transform the sun's elusive rays into a valuable—and safe—source of energy.

Send: a postcard

Ask for: "Solar Energy and You"

Write to: Renewable Energy Information
P.O. Box 8900
Silver Spring, MD 20907

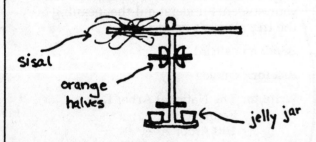

sisal

orange halves

jelly jar

American Wild Flowers Coloring Book

Wild flowers are more than just a beautiful part of the landscape. They are an important part of America's heritage, a part which is always threatened. This coloring book has 46 of the most important wild flowers, in illustrations taken from Rickett's collection. What children grow to know, they will surely come to value.

Send: $2.50 (plus $2.50 postage & handling)

Ask for: "American Wild Flowers Coloring Book"

Write to: Dover Publications, Inc.
31 East 2nd Street
Mineola, NY 11501

Pollution Pointers for Kids

This two-page flier offers 25 projects teachers can perform with their students that will make everyone involved more aware of pollution and the ways we can help solve pollution problems. Suggestions include a litter art show, fancy can displays, and pollution contests. Up to 5 free copies free.

Send: a postard (5¢ each for over 5 copies)

Ask for: "Pollution Pointers for Elementary Students"

Write to: Keep America Beautiful, Inc.
Communications Dept.
9 W. Broad St.
Stamford, CT 06902

Environmental Issues

The Sierra Club has a brand-new source-book which will be most helpful to the environmentally concerned educator. It gives a complete listing of all their publications and brochures, touching on a variety of environmental issues such as protecting wildlife, conservation, and general awareness. A copy may be obtained free by contacting the Sierra Club.

Send: a postcard

Ask for: "A Sourcebook"

Write to: Sierra Club
Public Affairs
730 Polk Street
San Francisco, CA 94109

Arbor Day Is Back in Style

Each issue of "Arbor Day News" is devoted to a different tree-related theme. For example, one issue discussed Arbor Day celebrations, offering ideas used by schools and communities around the country. It also included a detailed plan for a school Arbor Day celebration, complete with tree-planting instructions. The newsletter is clearly written and extremely informative, and the foundation people will send you a single copy free.

Send: a postcard

Ask for: "Arbor Day News"

Write to: The National Arbor Day
Foundation
100 Arbor Ave.
Nebraska City, NE 68410

Endangered Species

Greta Nilsson has written an invaluable comprehensive resource for every teacher who is concerned about endangered species. This 224-page illustrated book normally sells for $6.00, but teachers can obtain a copy at no charge. It contains projects for classrooms and science fairs which will help children gain an awareness of the danger which many species face and ways to preventing their extinction. For the older child, it suggests biology projects which are more humane than those ordinarily on schools' curricula.

Send: request on school's letterhead

Ask for: "The Endangered Species
Handbook"

Write to: Animal Welfare Institute
P.O. Box 3650
Washington, D.C. 20007

V. Health and Safety

HE LIMPS AND WALKS FUNNY-

Helping Youth Decide

Sooner or later, growing children are faced with such physically and emotionally dangerous issues as smoking, drinking, and even pressure at school and at home. Written for parents and teachers, this book offers suggestions on how to discuss these sensitive subjects warmly and openly. Single copies in Spanish and English are available for free.

Send: a postcard

Ask for: "Helping Youth Decide"

Write to: Peter Sparber & Assoc.
1325 Pennsylvania Ave., N.W.
Suite 500
Washington, D.C. 20004

Safety in the House

The number of accidents that occur each year in the home is overwhelming. Every year too many children are injured in accidents that could have easily been prevented. The National Easter Seal Society offers a checklist that can help parents make their homes safer for their children. Sending home this 3-fold leaflet—available in English or Spanish—with your students could make a difference in the welfare of the children in your class.

Send: 2 for $1.00

Ask for: A-210 "A Safe Home Is No Accident" or A-210S for a Spanish version

Write to: National Easter Seal Society
70 East Lake Street
Chicago, IL 60601

A Montessori Approach to Alcoholism

If the children of alcoholics are to break the alcoholic life-style that is perpetuated from generation to generation, it is imperative that they develop their potential for creativity, initiative, independence, inner discipline, and self-confidence. The Montessori approach is ideal for treating the children of alcoholics. In a booklet published by the American Montessori Society, the authors explain why this approach is so effective and offer a careful analysis of elements of an educational environment that would best suit the child of an alcoholic. An intelligent study, important for teachers and parents alike.

Send: $1.00

Ask for: X109 "Social Work in Family Life Enrichment: The Children of Alcoholics—A Montessori Approach"

Write to: American Montessori Society
150 Fifth Ave.
New York, NY 10011

Help Your Students Make the Most of Their Eyes

Teachers are in a unique position to observe and detect vision difficulties. In the classroom, students must concentrate on a multitude of tasks requiring both near and distance visual skills. Effective and efficient vision is related to academic achievement, and observant teachers can help avoid problems. The American Optometric Association offers a free brochure outlining indications of possible visual impairment.

Send: request on school letterhead and a self-addressed, stamped business-size envelope

Ask for: "A Teacher's Guide to Vision Problems"

Write to: Communications Center
Dept. FTT
American Optometric Association
243 N. Lindbergh Blvd.
St. Louis, MO 63141

Bicycle Safety

This clearly written pamphlet describes in detail what young cyclists should know about maintaining and caring for their bikes. It also describes rules for safe cycling and illustrates proper turn signals. A bit of bike trivia is offered in the back (at the turn of the century, most police departments had bike patrolmen who arrested 12-mile-an-hour speedsters). An important guide for any cyclist.

Send: 35¢ for 3

Ask for: "Bicycle Safety Tips"

Write to: The National Easter Seal Society
70 East Lake Street
Chicago, IL 60601

Schools Without Drugs

Today, unlike a few years ago, every school-age child will sooner or later have to make a decision about whether or not to use drugs for recreational purposes. The Consumer Information Center offers a straightforward primer for parents and teachers about children and drug abuse. It describes the extent of the problem, the effects of various drugs, and describes signs of use. It also includes a discussion of legal considerations and an extensive list of resources.

Send: a postcard

Ask for: "Schools Without Drugs" #511W

Write to: Consumer Information Center
P.O. Box 100
Pueblo, CO 81002

Don't Touch!

As part of its nationwide campaign to inform the public about the dangers of explosives, the Institute of Makers of Explosives offers schools a free-loan program for its "Don't Touch!" videotape. The video is full of information on explosives and describes, among other things, what to do if you find a commercial blasting cap. Safety posters and a booklet of helpful information to supplement the video are provided as well. Should your school wish to purchase the video, special arrangements to reproduce "Don't Touch!" can be made at considerably reduced costs.

Send: request on school letterhead

Ask for: "Don't Touch!"

Write to: Institute of Makers of Explosives
1575 Eye St., N.W., Suite 550
Washington, DC 20005

Help for Students of Alcoholic Families

Alcoholics Anonymous, an organization dedicated to helping alcoholics achieve and maintain sobriety, also helps family and friends deal with the baffling and at times violent irrationality of the alcoholic. A student with an alcoholic relative can suffer from severe emotional problems that interfere with his or her ability to learn. In the pamphlet "Is There an Alcoholic in Your Life?" A.A. offers elementary and stimulating information as well as down-to-earth suggestions on how to deal with the alcoholic and where to go for further help.

Send: 25¢

Ask for: P-30

Write to: A.A. World Services, Inc.
P.O. Box 459
Grand Central Station
New York, NY 10163

Learning About Poisons

In this amusing 16-page booklet offered by the Consumer Information Council, children can learn about poisonous substances with Dennis the Menace as their guide. He discusses the various poisons found around the home and how children can tell if something is safe to eat. An appropriate and useful guide.

Send: a postcard

Ask for: 504W "Dennis Takes a Poke at Poison"

Write to: Consumer Information Catalog
P.O. Box 100
Pueblo, CO 81002

Health Alert

Achoo. Just one sneeze and suddenly the whole class has it. The *Child Health Alert* is a monthly newsletter which provides an overview of current issues, research, and information commentary regarding all aspects of children's health. An excellent source of quick, up-to-date health information. Teachers can obtain a free sample copy by writing to the organization.

Send: a postcard

Ask for: "A free sample of *Child Health Alert*"

Write to: Child Health Alert
P.O. Box 338
Newton Highlands, MA 02161

AIDS Education

This 28-page, free booklet from the Consumer Information Catalog may be one of the most important pieces of information you ever bring into your classroom. It supplies facts about AIDS, its transmission, and talks about how teens are at risk. It also includes a description of methods of protection, guidelines for selecting educational materials, and sources for more information. This information is vital even if you work primarily with elementary-age children.

Send: a postcard

Ask for: 509W "AIDS and the Education of Our Children: A Guide for Parents and Teachers"

Write to: Consumer Information Catalog
P.O. Box 100
Pueblo, CO 81002

Sport Sense

With kids involved in so many varied and sophisticated sports, it is vital that they—as well as their parents and teachers—understand the increased nutritional needs of their athletically active bodies. Nancy Clark, nutritionist and author of "The Athlete's Kitchen," has written this common-sense approach pamphlet of nutritional tips for athletes. "Sport Sense" emphasizes the importance of exercise to good health, underlining the need to meet nutritional needs with carbohydrates and regular, well-balanced meals. Includes 5 well-balanced, tasty recipes.

Send: a self-addressed, stamped, business-size envelope

Ask for: "Sport Sense"

Write to: Rice Council for Market Development
Dept. "Sport Sense"
P.O. Box 740121
Houston, TX 77274

Posture Education

Reedco, "The Good Posture People," offers a reference sheet with suggestions and exercises for stimulating good posture in the classroom. By emphasizing good posture while standing, sitting, walking, lifting, and carrying, teachers may help prevent posture deformities and make the student a healthier person.

Send: a self-addressed, stamped envelope

Ask for: "Basic Posture Patterns and Distortions with Adapted Exercise Programs"

Write to: Reedco Research
51 N. Fulton St.
Auburn, NY 13021

Watersafe

This 17-minute release on basic water safety techniques is available for loan on color film or videocassette free of charge. Olympic swimming champion Donna de Varona demonstrates for viewers safety tactics and methods of coping with emergencies while engaged in water events.

Send: a postcard

Ask for: a brochure

Write to: Modern Talking Picture
Service
5000 Park St. N.
St. Petersburg, FL 33709

Young People and A.A.

As every educator is aware, teenage and preteenage drinking is on the rise. A.A., the nationwide organization of alcoholics who share their experience in the hope that they may solve their common problem and help others recover, publishes an excellent pamphlet titled "Young People and A.A." In it, each of 10 members, ages 16 to 27, tells his or her own story and describes how the program works. If there's a problem drinker in your class, this booklet may help him or her to get back on the right track.

Send: 30¢

Ask for: P-4

Write to: A.A. World Services, Inc.
P.O. Box 459
Grand Central Station
New York, NY 10163

And, if you do need help or if you'd just like to talk to someone about your drinking, call us. We're in the phone book under Alcoholics Anonymous.

VI. Mathematics

Safe Compass and Protractor

The Teachers Exchange of San Francisco has created a safe and fun paper compass/protractor which is perfect for teaching young children all about circles. The two-pencil compass works by putting the tip of one pencil into the hole marked "Center of the Circle" and the other at the length you choose the diameter to be (inches or centimeters)—then you draw your circle. The bookmark-shaped card has all the circle formulas, the number value for π, and an easy-to-use protractor (with instructions) on the back. The package of 30 includes enough for the whole class.

Send: $2.95 for 30 (plus $1.00 postage & handling)

Ask for: "The 2-Pencil Compass"

Write to: Teachers Exchange of San Francisco
28 Dawnview
San Francisco, CA 94131

What Is Basic in Mathematics?

What mathematics do all children need for their lives in a society that depends on technology? What do they need in order to go on and learn the math they will need for access to jobs in industry and business? These questions and many others are answered in a 45-page booklet written by Stephen Willoughby, director of mathematics education at New York University. Willoughby is dedicated to helping children learn the usefulness of math in solving the problems of their daily lives.

Send: $2.00 (plus $2.50 postage & handling)

Ask for: "Teaching Mathematics: What Is Basic?"

Write to: Council for Basic Education
725 15th St., N.W.
Washington, DC 20005

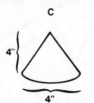

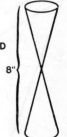

Fun with Numbers Coloring Book

What better way to teach counting and number skills? As children color these 45 charming illustrations, they will learn to count to twenty and perform simple addition and subtraction. Each scene teaches a basic lesson and is accompanied by a rhyme that helps children to remember the lesson.

Send: $2.50 (plus $2.50 postage & handling)

Ask for: "Fun with Numbers Coloring Book"

Write to: Dover Publications
31 E. 2nd St.
Mineola, NY 11501

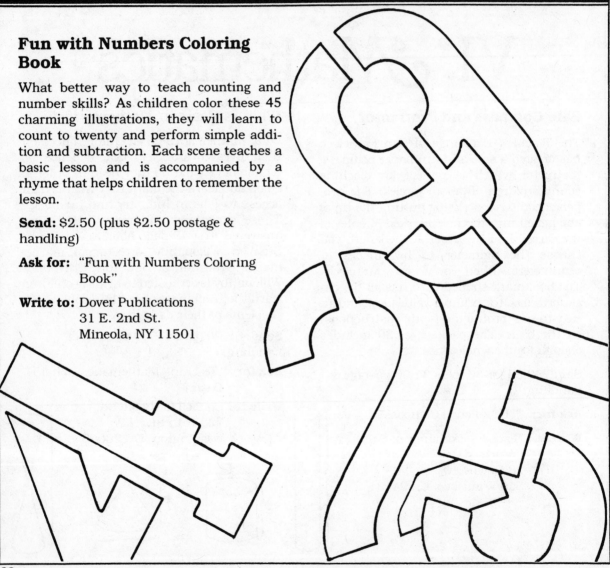

Numbers for Beginners

"The Little Numbers Coloring Book" teaches children counting and simple arithmetic as they color bunnies, snowmen, kittens, and more. This book contains over thirty exercises, each one designed to convey some lesson of mathematical import.

Send: $1.00 (plus $2.50 postage & handling)

Ask for: "The Little Numbers Coloring Book"

Write to: Dover Publications, Inc.
31 East 2nd Street
Mineola, NY 11501

Elementary Math

For serious math teachers only: a five-part discussion of elementary math curriculum and how it can and should be improved. This 20-page paper could entirely change the way you think about teaching math.

Send: $3.00

Ask for: "On Mathematicians in Curriculum Reform in Elementary Mathematics" (Elementary Subjects Center Series No. 9)

Mastering 2 + 2

National test scores are down, particularly on items that deal with problem solving or with the ability to use math in real situations. The Cuisenaire Co. believes that the solution lies not in inventing new materials, but rather in making better use of the materials that have proven effective in the past. They claim that teachers who incorporate their manipulative material have a greater chance of producing math and science achievers than teachers who do not. Activities include Base Ten, Pattern Blocks, Connecting Cubes, science kits, and staff development videotapes.

Send: a postcard

Ask for: catalog

Write to: Cuisenaire Co. of America, Inc.
12 Church St.
New Rochelle, NY 10802

VII. Music

Rethinking Music

In this 31-page paper, author R. L. Erbes reviews the nature of higher-order thinking by comparing the concepts of creative thinking and critical thinking in the context of teaching elementary music. The author contends that music should continue to be treated as an art and students must not only become knowledgeable about music, but must also learn to think intelligently about music. An appendix gives a detailed analysis of a typical general music lesson.

Send: $3.25

Ask for: "Elementary General Music: A Discipline-Based Review" (Elementary Subjects Center Series No. 4)

Write to: IRT Publications
Michigan State University
252 Erickson Hall
East Lansing, MI 48824-1034

EasyReeding

Do you know how many presidents have played the harmonica? What was the first musical instrument played in outer space? What musical instrument did Benjamin Franklin invent? Hohner's new 16-page booklet on harmonicas—spiced throughout with numerous little-known fun facts—covers the history and production of harmonicas.

Send: a self-addressed, stamped legal-size envelope

Ask for: "EasyReeding"

Write to: Hohner, Inc.
Dept. FTT-1
P.O. Box 15035
Richmond, VA 23227

Rainbow Harmonica

This is probably the simplest harmonica learning system ever devised! In only minutes your students will be playing songs they know and like. The Rainbow's color-coded harmonica and song book work together to teach children to play music and enjoy the harmonica. The redesigned harmonica has only 4 holes (8 notes) for one complete octave. The 32-page instruction and music book uses a three-step system, starting with color-coded arrows and ending with musical notations. The harmonica and book are available only to teachers in a special pre-introduction offer.

Send: $5.00

Ask for: "Rainbow Harmonica and Instruction System"

Write to: Hohner Inc.
Dept. Rainbow
P.O. Box 9375
Richmond, VA
23227

Music Austrian Style

From this colorful fold-out printed by the Austrian Press and Information Service, you and your students will learn about Minnesingers, Viennese opera composers, and contemporary Austrian musicians. Brief but informative biographies of Mozart, Haydn, the Strausses, Schönberg, Mahler, Bruckner, Berg, Hauer, Schubert, and Wolf are also included. The fold-out is attractively designed and shows photos of various musically related items, including Beethoven's death mask, a program from *The Magic Flute*, and an ink drawing of the stage design for the 1975 Bregenz Festival. A fascinating way to introduce the world of Austrian music to students.

Send: a postcard

Ask for: "Austria Music"

Write to: Austrian Press and Information Service
31 E. 69th St.
New York, NY 10021

Singing Games

Noted American folklorist Richard Chase presents 18 traditional games complete with tunes and instructions. This fully illustrated book is filled with games—singing and other types—that are perfect for class parties or simply a fun break. The book includes favorites such as Turn the Glasses Over, and In and Out the Window, as well as new games that are sure to please.

Send: $2.50 (Plus $2.50 postage & handling)

Ask for: "Singing Games and Playparty Games"

Write to: Dover Publications, Inc.
31 East 2nd Street
Mineola, NY 11501

VIII. Nutrition

Beyond Patty-Cake

Teaching children to cook is more than just fun—it provides them with a useful skill that will help them fend for themselves when they grow older. *More Than Graham Crackers: Nutrition Education and Food Preparation with Young Children* is a book which provides lots of delicious and nutritious recipes along with finger plays and other teaching ideas to help children learn to prepare good food. Definitely the last word in classroom cooking.

Send: $4.00

Ask for: "More Than Graham Crackers: Nutrition Education and Food Preparation with Young Children"

Write to: National Association for the Education of Young Children 1834 Connecticut Avenue, N.W. Washington, DC 20009-5786

Fat Facts

More and more information is coming to light every day about fat and its connection to cancer risk. By informing yourself, you are not only helping yourself, but you can use your knowledge to inform your students and their parents as well. So get all the facts from the source, a free brochure from the American Institute for Cancer Research.

Send: a postcard

Ask for: "All About Fat and Cancer Risk"

Write to: American Institute for Cancer Research Dept. FC2 Washington, D.C. 20069

Dietary Guidelines

Are you prepared to start your students on the way to a lifetime of good eating habits? If not, the USDA has made it easy for you. They publish a set of seven dietary guidelines to help you and your students stay healthy based on nutrition research. The booklet includes charts on desirable body weights and caloric expenditures for various exercises and activities.

Send: 50¢

Ask for: "Dietary Guidelines for Americans" 420W

Write to: Consumer Information Center
P.O. Box 100
Pueblo, Colorado 81002

An Apple for the Teacher

Fruit is a wonderful thing. Fruits are nutritious, easy to prepare, and they taste great! This free booklet tells you all about fruits, their nutritious benefits, and how to minimize vitamin loss in cooking. Now your students will know that when they give you an apple, they're not only telling you how much they like and value you, they're also wishing you good health!

Send: a postcard

Ask for: "Fruit: Something Good That's Not Illegal, Immoral or Fattening" 524W

Write to: Consumer Information Center
P.O. Box 100
Pueblo, Colorado 81002

THE PEANUT WIZARD
GEORGE WASHINGTON CARVER

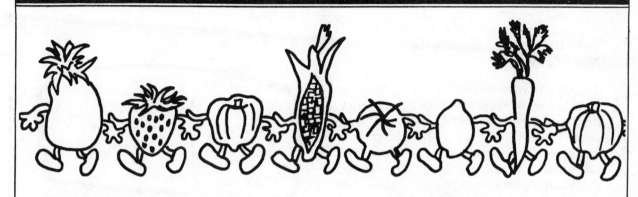

Fun Food Groups

It's never too early to learn about good nutrition! These four colorful posters help very young children become familiar with the four basic food groups: Fruits and Vegetables, Proteins, Grains, and Dairy Products. These 12″ × 16″ posters are printed on sturdy coated stock and come in a handy plastic storage envelope.

Send: $3.95 for all four

Ask for: "Nutrition Poster Set"

Write to: Troll Associates
Early Childhood Materials
100 Corporate Drive
Mahwah, NJ 07430

Packing Brown Bags with Nutrition

There's no reason children who have to "brown-bag it" should be deprived of nutritious foods, and this booklet makes packing healthy lunches a breeze. It includes recipes and ideas for creative hot and cold lunches and a chart listing calories, fat, cholesterol, and sodium contents in popular snacks. Order a pamphlet and send it home with your little brown-baggers.

Send: $2.50

Ask for: 124W "Making Bag Lunches, Snacks, and Desserts"

Write to: Consumer Information Center
P.O. Box 100
Pueblo, Colorado 81002

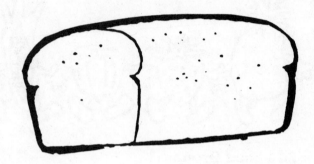

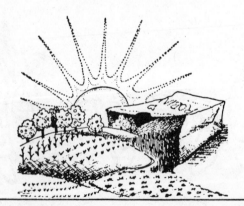

How Is Bread Made?

"Bread in the Making," a colorfully illustrated booklet published by the American Institute of Baking, takes readers on a tour of a bread factory. Mr. Blake, their guide, talks about ingredients, mixing, dividing and rounding, proofing, depanning, cooling, slicing, wrapping, and delivering. Fun for children to read alone or in groups.

Send: 50¢

Ask for: "Bread in the Making"

Write to: American Institute of Baking
Communications Dept.
1213 Bakers Way
Manhattan, KS 66502

Rice Plus

Rice is one of the oldest sources of food in the world, having been cultivated since 2800 B.C.! "Facts About US Rice," published by the Rice Council, describes the history and production of rice in the United States, explaining how rice is still an important nutritional staple today. "Eat Smart" includes several delicious recipes for rice, while "Brown Rice" supplies additional recipes and information.

Send: a self-addressed, stamped business-size envelope

Ask for: booklet by name

Write to: Rice Council for Market
Development
Dept. (name of booklet)
P.O. Box 74012
Houston, TX 77274

Nutrition Tables

Are you trying to teach your students about nutrition? Well, here's a visual aid that just can't be beat. Tables giving nutritive values of more than 900 common foods, including information on calories, sodium, calcium, cholesterol, vitamins, RDA's and more. Seventy-two pages of pure fact.

Send: $2.75

Ask for: "Nutritive Value of Foods" 120W

Write to: Consumer Information Center
P.O. Box 100
Pueblo, Colorado 81002

IX. Parents and Community

Community Cleanup

A cleanup campaign is a good way of improving the local environment, but to be effective, it takes planning. Keep America Beautiful's outline spells it out for you and tells you the government officials to contact, how to prepare a grid map of a community for cleanup-crew assignments, how to recruit volunteers, how to secure the cooperation of business and industry, how to publicize the campaign, how to co-ordinate volunteers, and the necessary follow-up tasks. Up to 5 copies free.

Send: a postcard (5¢ each for over 5 copies)

Write to: Keep America Beautiful, Inc.
Communications Dept.
9 W. Broad St.
Stamford, CT 06902

School Support for Stepfamilies

The Stepfamily Association of America Inc. is offering a kit which includes a booklet entitled "Support for Stepfamilies: Suggestions for Schools," a brochure of the programs offered by the association, information about SHAPES (a school program for children of stepfamilies), and a copy of "Stepfamilies," the association's quarterly publication.

Send: $4.00

Ask for: "School Information Packet"

Write to: Stepfamily Association of America
215 Centennial Mall South
Suite 212
Lincoln, NB 68508

Merrily We Roll Along

Taking young children on long car trips—or even short ones!—can be quite an adventure. So J. B. McCracken came up with a bunch of ways to keep children busy while they are buckled up, and is willing to share them. This brochure from the National Association for the Education of Young Children will be in constant demand from the parents of your students, if not for those in your class, for their younger siblings!

Send: 50¢

Ask for: "Merrily We Roll Along"

Write to: National Association for the
Education of Young Children
1834 Connecticut Avenue, N.W.
Washington, DC 20009-5786

School Crime

During World War II and the 1950s, crime and delinquency rates remained relatively stable, but by the 1960s, the rate of crime increased to a point where it demanded public concern. The ERIC fact sheet on school crime and disruption discusses the extent of violence in the schools, the relationship between school crime and the community, and the action schools can take to create a safe and secure learning environment.

Send: a postcard

Ask for: Fact Sheet Number 1

Write to: ERIC Clearinghouse on
Urban Education
Box 40
Teachers College
Columbia University
New York, NY 10027

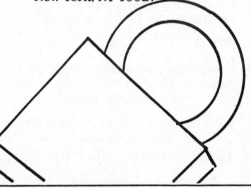

The Community School and Montessori

The community-school concept can be traced back to Plato and is based on the idea that learning is a lifelong process that does not end with a diploma. The Montessori approach promotes the idea that the child carries within him the potentialities of the person he will become. One of the basic premises of the Montessori method is that freedom to develop is achieved through the development of order and self-discipline. Both approaches aim for self attainment. In a booklet published by the American Montessori Society, the authors outline the fundamental principles of these two approaches and describe possible methods of implementation.

Send: $1.00

Ask for: X103 "A Montessori Program in a Community School System"

Write to: American Montessori Society
150 Fifth Ave.
New York, NY 10011

Family Reading

Reading together not only has a marked impact upon a child's grades and learning ability, but it has also been shown to improve the emotional well-being of the entire family. Reading Is Fundamental Inc. distributes a number of brochures to give parents (and teachers) practical tips to encourage family reading, and each brochure is only 50¢. Send one home to your kid's parents and put the fun back into fundamental.

Send: a postcard

Ask for: "List of Brochures"

Write to: Reading Is Fundamental
600 Maryland Avenue, Suite 500
Washington, DC 20024

Growing Without Schooling

"Growing Without Schooling" is a bi-monthly magazine for people who have taken or wish to take their children out of school and have them learn at home. It includes articles by John Holt and other renowned educators, legal information, learning resources, advice from parents, and a copy of Holt's mail-order book list.

Send: $3.50

Ask for: sample of "Growing Without Schooling"

Write to: "Growing Without Schooling"
2269 Massachusetts Ave.
Cambridge, MA 02140

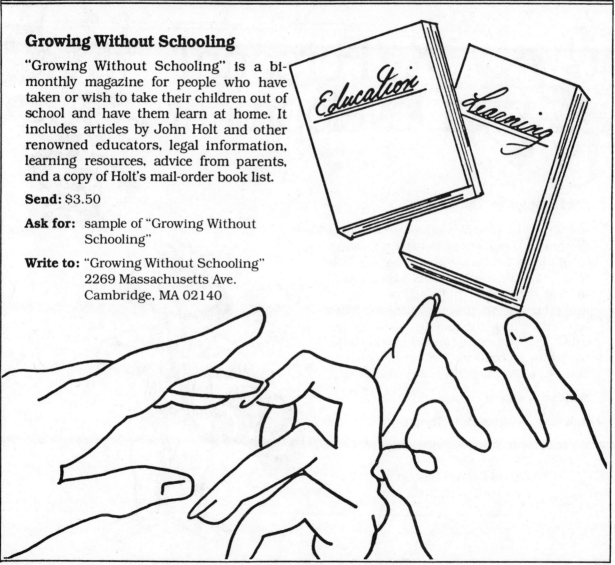

X. Personal Development

A Message to Teenagers

A.A. provides a simple twelve-question quiz designed to help teenagers determine when drinking is becoming a problem. As any teacher knows, alcoholism is a rough word to deal with. Most high school students are reluctant to discuss drinking with teachers, whom they see as authority figures. This pamphlet can help by allowing teenagers to confront their own problem, and tells them where they can go to get help.

Send: a postcard

Ask for: "A Message to Teenagers"

Write to: A.A. World Services, Inc.
P.O. Box 459
Grand Central Station
New York, NY 10163

Developing Humane Attitudes

An interest in and fondness for animal life is apparently a part of every child and it is during childhood and youth that the greatest good can be accomplished in instilling a knowledge of animals and an interest in our interdependence with animals.

The Animal Welfare Institute publishes a book that tells the instructor how to teach children about first aid and care of mice, gerbils, rabbits, birds, opossums, and other small animals. Single copies free.

Send: request on school letterhead

Ask for: "First Aid and Care of Small Animals"

Write to: Animal Welfare Institute
P.O. Box 3650
Washington, DC 20007

Supporting Children's Growth

Caring *can* make a difference. In this book by R.M. Warren, you'll find positive ways to help children deal with difficult issues such as divorce, abuse, and death.

Send: $4.00

Ask for: "Caring: Supporting Children's Growth" (NAEYC no. 213)

Write to: National Association for the Education of Young Children
1834 Connecticut Ave., N.W.
Washington, DC 20009

Braille for Seeing Children

Did you ever shut your eyes and run your fingers over a page of Braille printing? All the little raised dots seem to run together. Even if you knew the Braille alphabet, your fingers could not pick out each separate dot. But boys and girls who cannot see read stories in Braille. Their fingers are trained to be their eyes.

A special Braille edition of "My Weekly Reader" has been prepared by the American Printing House for the Blind so that seeing children may better understand how their blind friends see and write. Up to 5 copies free.

Send: a postcard (35¢ each for over 5 copies)

Ask for: "My Weekly Reader"

Write to: American Printing House for the
Blind
1839 Frankfort Ave.
Louisville, KY 40206

Teaching Children to Care

Suppose an enormous lion suddenly appeared right in front of you, what would you do? Well, there probably wouldn't be much you could do except sit tight and hope that he was a good kind lion. And that's pretty well what all smaller creatures have to do when you suddenly appear in front of them—they all just hope that you are a good kind lion too.

In this delightfully illustrated pamphlet, the Animal Welfare Institute requests that children be good kind lions to birds, polliwogs, mice, rabbits, butterflies, and other small creatures. Single copies free.

Send: a self-addressed, stamped envelope

Ask for: "Good Kind Lion"

Write to: Animal Welfare Institute
P.O. Box 3650
Washington, DC 20007

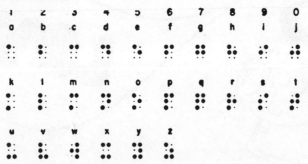

Great Great Grandmother

Great Grand Father

Great Grandmother

Family Tree Workbook

Central to a child's world are the self and the family. Because of this innocent egocentricity, nothing could be more fascinating than tracing the how, why, where, and who of themselves. "My Family Tree Workbook" is an easy-to-use introduction to genealogy designed especially for children. Data pages for recording name, birthdate, place of birth, occupation, and other facts, as well as space for a photograph, are provided for great-grandparents, grandparents, parents, siblings, and the child. In addition, the author offers suggestions on collecting data, obtaining civil and church records, and tracing immigrant ancestors.

Grand Father

Grandmother Grandmother

Father mother

Child child

Send: $2.50 (plus $2.50 postage & handling)

Ask for: "My Family Tree Workbook"

Write to: Dover Publications, Inc.
31 E. 2nd St.
Mineola, NY 11501

XI. Publication Catalogs, Films, and Other A-V Aids

Toward a Bias-Free Society

The Council on Interracial Books for Children is dedicated to countering racism, sexism, and other forms of bias that children are habitually exposed to. Their catalog is free of charge and lists numerous filmstrips, books, pamphlets, lesson plans, and other curricula concerning issues of equality in school and society.

Send: a postcard

Ask for: catalog of publications

Write to: Council on Interracial Books
CIBC Resource Center
1841 Broadway
New York, NY 10023

Library of Congress

The Library of Congress is a resource every teacher should know about. Its stacks hold over 18 million books and pamphlets as well as newspapers, magazines, photographs, manuscripts, maps, posters, prints, films, television tapes, records, and lots more. The catalog lists books, pamphlets, serials, music, and literary recordings.

Send: a postcard

Ask for: "Publications in Print"

Write to: Library of Congress
Office Systems Services
Printing and Processing Section
Washington, DC 20540

Reusable Text-Workbooks

Ann Arbor Publishers, the people who make reusable, nonconsumable text-workbooks, offer a wealth of materials for the teacher, including resource kits, arithmetic handbooks, ABC mazes, art activities, and many social and psychological aids, including a book on self-understanding and one on the need to fail. A valuable list.

Send: a postcard

Ask for: "Publications"

Write to: Ann Arbor Publishers, Inc.
20 Commercial Blvd.
Novato, CA 94949

Catalog of A-V Materials

Troll Associates, well known for their educational publications and children's book clubs, also provides films, slides, tapes, and countless other A-V materials on a wide variety of subjects. Teachers can get a copy of Troll's A-V catalog for free if it is delivered directly to their school.

Send: a postcard

Ask for: Catalog of A-V Materials

Write to: Troll Associates
100 Corporate Dr.
Mahwah, NJ 07430

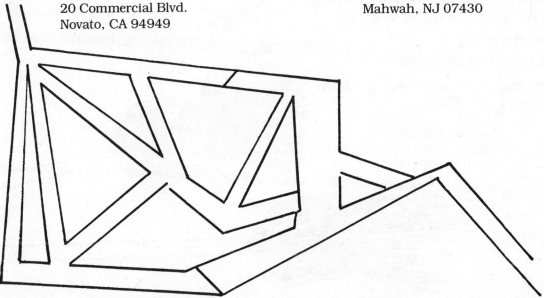

Clearinghouse on Urban Education

ERIC stands for the Educational Resources Information Center. It is designed to provide users with ready access to primarily English-language literature dealing with education. ERIC's publications on urban education deal with topics such as decentralization, ethnicity, motivation, dropouts, human relations, learning patterns in the disadvantaged, and trends in bilingual education. The catalog includes an extensive list of annotated bibliographies and commissioned papers. Well worthwhile for any teacher trying to keep up to date.

Send: a postcard

Ask for: list of publications

Write to: ERIC Clearinghouse on Urban
Education
Box 40
Teachers College
Columbia University
New York, NY 10027

Great Kids' Books

Workman Publishing offers a wealth of exciting books for kids, including "Snips & Snails & Walnut Whales," "Steven Caney's Toy Book," and "The Boy and the Dove," the enchanting tale of a boy and his pet who must part, but who nevertheless find a new way of being together. Check out their catalog for books on crafts, hobbies, sports, and cooking.

Send: a postcard

Ask for: catalog

Write to: Workman Publishing Co., Inc.
708 Broadway
New York, NY 10018

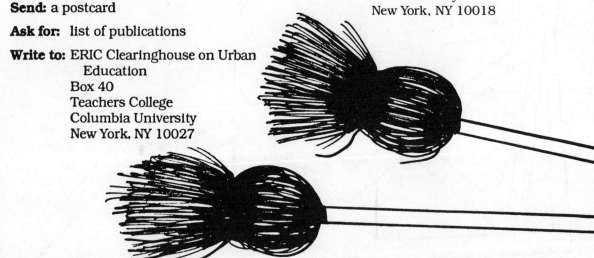

Consumer Information Catalog

This catalog is a wealth of information, listing a selection of federal publications that could be of interest to teachers. Everything from food to education, from money management to travel and hobbies, is listed in this booklet. And best of all, almost everything is under $6.00, with many items free! Educators can also be put on a mailing list if they wish to receive 25 copies or more for their schools or libraries.

Send: a postcard

Ask for: Consumer Information Catalog

Write to: Consumer Information Center
P.O. Box 100
Pueblo, CO 81002

Give Them the Big Picture

Giant Photos offers full-color posters and prints, most of which are available for $2.00. Teachers can bring their classrooms to life with scenes from China, Japan or Switzerland; or illustrated versions of Patrick Henry's speech or the Preamble to the Declaration of Independence. A wide variety of sports and animal posters is also available.

Send: a postcard

Ask for: free catalog

Write to: Giant Photos, Inc.
P.O. Box 406
Rockford, IL 61105

Soft Spaces

Environments Inc. offers two free publications which should be especially helpful for the teachers of grades K-2. "Environments Planning Kits" contains giant grids and press-apply equipment cutouts to create your own custom layout. "Environments Early Childhood Equipment and Materials Guide" is a 192-page catalog which has materials for early education and child-care programs.

Send: a postcard

Ask for: "Environments Planning Kits" or "Environments Early Childhood Equipment and Materials Guide"

Write to: Environments, Inc.
P.O. Box 1348
Beaufort, SC 29901-1348

Free-Loan Educational Films

One of the country's largest distributors of free-loan films and videocassettes offers a catalog of their program available for many categories, e.g., energy and ecology, health and hygiene, home economics, safety and auto, science and technology, and more. Users pay return postage only on 16mm films. Postage is prepaid on videocassettes.

Send: a postcard

Ask for: catalog of free-loan educational films/videos. Please indicate grade level

Write to: Modern Talking Picture Service
5000 Park St., N.
St. Petersburg, FL 33709

Info on Science, Math, and Environmental Ed.

The ERIC Clearinghouse for Science, Mathematics, and Environmental Education has processed several thousand documents and journal articles related to science, math, and environmental education. The materials include curriculum guides, research reports, evaluation reports, teacher's guides, and descriptions of educational and research programs. The annual bulletin and publications lists detail their activities and the information bulletins available.

Send: a postcard

Ask for: annual bulletin and publications lists

Write to: ERIC/SMEAC
Ohio State University
1200 Chambers Rd., Rm. 310
Columbus, OH 43212

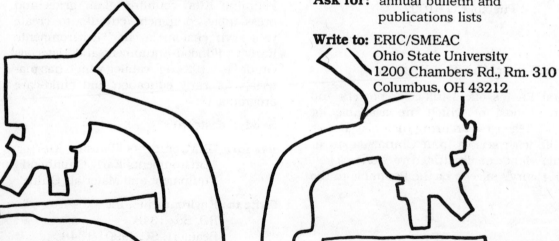

Unusual Teaching Aids

The Children's Book and Music Center is a unique source of phonograph records, cassettes, books, videos, rhythm instruments, and enrichment materials suitable for children and teachers. The materials offered were chosen by trained professionals and represent the best available for all areas of curriculum.

Send: $1.00

Ask for: catalog

Write to: Children's Book & Music Center
2500 Santa Monica Blvd.
Santa Monica, CA 90404

University Prints

The University Prints offers hundreds of study sets in a wide range of subjects, most of which are priced at 30 illustrations for $2.00. Set titles include "Visits to Many Lands," "Visits to Famous Cities," "Visits to Great Museums," "Visits to Notable Eras," "Saints and Apostles," "Famous Churches and Cathedrals," "Fine Arts and Architecture," "History and Social Studies," "Epic Poetry," "Costumes of Many Lands," "Greek and Roman Theatres," and many more. All prints are 5½″ by 8″. This brochure will tell you the history of the collection and lists the subject areas that are available.

Send: a postcard

Ask for: "Brochure: Special Topic Study
Sets"

Write to: The University Prints
21 East St.
P.O. Box 485
Winchester, MA 01890

Barron's

Although primarily known for their test preparation manuals and workbooks, Barron's also has a significant list of juvenile educational books, many of which cost under $5.00. Of special note are books done in collaboration with the renowned Bank Street College and Barron's wonderfully illustrated books on the four elements and the five senses.

Send: a postcard

Ask for: catalog of publications

Write to: Barron's
P.O. Box 8040
250 Wireless Blvd.
Haupauge, N.Y. 11788

Books and Computer Programs

Milliken Publishing Company not only publishes an excellent list of supplementary educational materials and equally wonderful early-childhood books, but they also have an entire catalog of computer software specifically designed for classrooms. Any or all of these catalogs can be ordered directly from Milliken. So, if you are interested in learning what big books, whole language materials, workbooks, transparencies, children's literature, reproducibles, or computer programs they have, just write.

Send: a postcard

Ask for: a catalog (specify type or all)

Write to: Milliken Publishing Company
1100 Research Blvd.
P.O. Box 21579
St. Louis, MO 63132-0579

XII. Reading, Writing, and Language

News for You

New Readers Press offers "News for You," a weekly newspaper written in easy English for adults and children. Designed like a newspaper, it includes national and international news, legal and consumer tips, profiles of prominent people, sports coverage, and a 4-page worksheet to test your knowledge. Also, throughout the school year, a monthly supplement gives in-depth coverage of current topics. The paper is perfect for stimulating reluctant readers.

Send: a postcard

Ask for: "News for You" sample and "Instructor's Aid"

Write to: New Readers Press
1320 Jamesville Ave., Box 131
Syracuse, NY 13210

Write Your Own Story Coloring Book

This book presents 23 full-page illustrations for children to color, plus room for them to write in their own stories about the adventures of Penny, Mark, and Koko the clown. Each page can be a separate story, or they can be connected to make one long story.

Send: $2.50 (plus $2.50 postage & handling)

Ask for: "Write Your Own Story Coloring Book"

Write to: Dover Publications, Inc.
31 E. 2nd St.
Mineola, NY 11501

Phonics in Beginning Reading

It's a fact: Some approaches to teaching reading are better than others, and it's also well known that children learn to read more readily when they are taught by sound and rational methods. In its booklet on phonics and beginning reading, the Council for Basic Education describes the history of past follies in reading theory and practice, but its primary purpose is to inform teachers of the superiority of phonics- or code-based approaches over the whole-word method. A well-researched and valuable discussion.

Send: $2.00 (plus $2.50 postage & handling)

Ask for: "Phonics in Beginning Reading"

Write to: Council for Basic Education
725 15th St., N.W.
Washington, DC 20005

Short **a** says **ă** in apple

Short **e** says **ĕ** in elephant

Short **I** says **Ī** in Indian

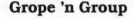

Grope 'n Group

These are word-classification cards, utilizing words found in basic texts. Please request by grade level (A=1st, B=2nd, etc.). Each set includes 15 cards except A, which includes 30.

Send: $4.00 for Set A; $2.00 for each of the others (plus $1.00 shipping & handling per order)

Ask for: "Grope 'n Group Set A" (or B, C, D, E, or F)

Write to: Teachers Exchange of San Francisco
28 Dawnview
San Francisco, CA 94131

Word-Detecto Cards

This hidden-word puzzle game includes 16 cards, each with different groups of letters printed on it. From each group, the student must find as many words of three or more letters as he or she can. Suitable for grades three to six.

Send: $1.50 (plus $1.00 postage & handling)

Ask for: Word-Detecto Cards

Write to: Teachers Exchange of San Francisco
28 Dawnview
San Francisco, CA 94131

Hidden Messages

This fascinating publication teaches children in the 5th grade and up how to spot sexism, racism, materialism, and elitism in even the simplest stories. Package includes a fun lesson on "The Princess and the Pea," a student handout, a complete lesson plan, and explanatory pamphlets.

Send: $3.00

Ask for: "Hidden Messages in Children's Stories"

Write to: Council on Interracial Books
CIBC Resource Center
1841 Broadway
New York, NY 10023

Teaching Inner-City Kids to Read

By studying four schools that have successfully taught city kids to read, George Weber, associate director for the Council for Basic Education, has concluded that the failure that characterizes beginning readers in inner-city schools is the fault of the schools, not the children. The factors that account for the success of the four schools are strong leadership, high expectations, good atmosphere, strong emphasis on reading, additional reading personnel, use of phonics, individualization, and careful evaluation of pupil progress. Weber elaborates on his findings in this welcome 37-page booklet.

Send: $2.00 (plus $2.50 postage & handling)

Ask for: "Inner-City Children Can Be Taught to Read"

Write to: Council for Basic Education
725 15th St., N.W.
Washington, DC 20005

Using the Library

The library is the most important resource a young student has. It provides a wealth of knowledge for papers, books for story times, and a place to sit quietly and study. The Consumer Information Center offers the publication "Helping Your Child Use the Library" to familiarize teachers with the various programs for children offered at most libraries. It also has a list of activities available for those children who have special needs.

Send: 50¢

Ask for: #412W "Helping Your Child Use the Library"

Write to: Consumer Information Center
P.O. Box 100
Pueblo, CO 81009

Title Twister

The Title Twister card is a creative writing teacher's dream. The inner circle lists personalities: "me, myself, and I," "the mad scientist," "Uncle Grouch," and many more. The outer circle lists situations: "a wild, wild adventure with...," "one day in the life of...," "a narrow escape...," and many others. Kids can mix and match over 400 combinations. Sure to set young imaginations on fire.

Send: $1.00 each title (plus $1.00 postage & handling)

Ask for: Title Twister or Title Twister II

Write to: Teachers Exchange of San Francisco
28 Dawnview
San Francisco, CA 94131

Why Teach Grammar?

Every native dialect reflects and perpetuates a local culture, and every student has the right to cherish that language and culture. But because a dialect represents just that, a local or limited culture, its value is bounded by its cultural milieu. If children are to understand, profit by, and contribute to the total culture of America, they must master the basic units of the language that we share. A child has a right to his own language, but he also has the right to know about the larger world in which he lives. These ideas and others are explicated in this formidable 42-page paper written by Kenneth Oliver, professor of English and comparative literature.

Send: $2.00 (plus $2.50 postage & handling)

Ask for: "A Sound Curriculum in English Grammar: Guidelines for Teachers and Parents"

Write to: Council for Basic Education
725 15th St., N.W.
Washington, DC 20005

Crossword Fun for Learning

The Teachers Exchange of San Francisco, specialists in innovative learning projects, now offers this package of 15 illustrated crossword puzzles for the intermediate grades. A protective coating for use with felt pens or crayons makes these puzzles reusable. Set A is for 4th- to 6th-graders, while set B is for use with 3rd- to 4th-graders. Helpful worksheets are also provided.

Send: $1.95 (plus $1.00 postage & handling)

Ask for: "Crossword Tasks" (specify set A or B)

Write to: Teachers Exchange of San Francisco
28 Dawnview
San Francisco, CA 94131

Turning Children into Readers

Enticing a child to read can be difficult in today's world of distractions. Whether it's watching television, playing video games, or just going outside to play, children can often think of a million things to do other than reading. To encourage your children to read, the International Reading Association has put out a series of booklets to help parents and teachers get children reading. The series includes: "How Can I Prepare My Young Child for Reading?" (No. 163), "Helping Your Child Become A Reader" (No. 161), and "You Can Help Your Young Child with Writing" (No. 160).

Send: $1.75 for each booklet

Ask for: title and number of booklet

Write to: International Reading
Association
Dept. L89
800 Barksdale Rd.
P.O. Box 8139
Newark, DE
19714-8139

XIII. Science

Jungle World!

For grades 4–12, this 48-page book is designed to accompany the Jungle World exhibit at the Bronx Zoo. Fully illustrated, with a glossary and bibliography for students and teachers, "Tropical Asian Animals" brings the wonderful Jungle World experience to the classroom.

Send: $3.60

Ask for: "Tropical Asian Animals"

Write to: Education Department
New York Zoological Society
Bronx Zoo
Bronx, NY 10460

Ornitholestes the Bird Robber

Ornitholestes (also called Coelurus) was one of the largest coelosaurs, somewhat larger than a man, but not nearly as heavy. He was capable of great speed and had sharp, hooked claws. Ornitholestes ("bird robber") lived during the Jurassic Period, and is thought to have fed upon small reptiles and early birds.

This carefully researched coloring book includes over 40 drawings of dinosaurs, archosaurs, fossil birds, and sea turtles. Each illustration is accompanied by an informative caption.

Send: $2.50 (plus $2.50 postage & handling)

Ask for: "The Dinosaur Coloring Book"

Write to: Dover Publications, Inc.
31 E. 2nd St.
Mineola, NY 11501

How to Forecast the Weather

Just watch the clouds, note the wind direction, and read the information on this chart, and you will be able to forecast the weather. The study of morning and evening skies can become an interesting hobby, and by comparing what you see in this chart, you and your students can become amateur weather prophets.

Send: $2.00 (each)

Ask for: Chart B (6th grade and up)
Chart C (grades 3–5)

Write to: Cloud Chart, Inc.
P.O. Box 21298
Charleston, SC 29413

Space Photos

Space Photos of Houston, Texas, will send you slides of outer space as seen through the eyes of the cameras on the various Apollo, Voyager, Viking, and Mariner missions. These slides, photos, posters, postcards, and prints document one of the most thrilling eras in recent history: man's conquest of space. Space Photos also supplies commemorative coins, covers, and emblems. Simply perusing the catalog is an educational experience.

Send: $2.50

Ask for: catalog

Write to: Space Photos
2608 Sunset Blvd.
Houston, TX 77005

Star Gazing

Astronomy is a wonderful subject for children to study as they have one of its most important resources at their disposal every evening: the nighttime sky. "Stars in Your Eyes: A Guide to the Northern Skies" is a great way to teach your students about the constellations. This booklet tells where to find many constellations as well as how they got their names.

Send: $1.50

Ask for: 155W "Stars in Your Eyes: A Guide to the Northern Skies"

Write to: Consumer Information Catalog
P.O. Box 100
Pueblo, CO 81002

Mini-Planetarium Kit

Created by Louis Finsand of the University of North Iowa, this hand-held mini-planetarium can be used to teach astronomy to any grade level. Included with the space dome are complete assembly and use instructions as well as teaching ideas and directions on how to plot your zenith and northern horizon.

Send: $1.29 (plus $2.00 postage & handling)

Ask for: "Planetarium Kit" #MS-38/1

Write to: National Science Teachers Association
Publications Dept. PL
1742 Connecticut Avenue, NW
Washington, DC 20009-1171

For Curious Naturalists

The Curious Naturalist was a magazine which came out originally in the 1970s, but is no longer circulated. The Massachusetts Audubon Society offers reprints of *Naturalist* issues for between 50¢ and $1.00, and will send you a list of the reprints for free. The reprints contain activities one can do as well as guides to different flora and fauna. Issues available cover: leaf fall and color change; once upon a corn patch (field succession); animal families; stop pollution—breathe easier; how to keep warm—and cool; signs of spring; and many more.

Send: a postcard

Ask for: "Curious Naturalist Reprints List"

Write to: Massachusetts Audubon Society
Educational Resources
South Great Road
Lincoln, MA 01773

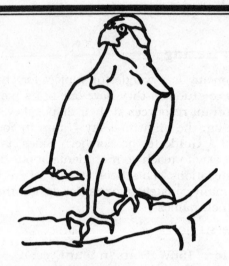

Trees of Arkansas

The detailed descriptions and line drawings in this unique book will teach students about the many native and ornamental trees of Arkansas. Tips for distinguishing trees by bark, leaves, flowers, fruit, and wood can serve as the basis for fun and educational classroom projects.

Send: $2.00 and purchase order number

Ask for: "Trees of Arkansas," by Dwight M. Moore

Write to: Arkansas Forestry Commission
1 & E Office
P.O. Box 4523
Asher Station
Little Rock, AR 72214

What Should Science Teachers Teach?

Children are very curious about the world in which they live. They are attracted to living things and fascinated by explanations—if the explainer knows how to retain the inherent interest in the phenomenon. In his 45-page paper, Dr. Howard J. Hausman, a member of the Council for Basic Education, describes ways to stimulate a child's curiosity and elaborates on his opinion that science should teach more than just facts and mechanical skills.

Send: $2.00 (plus $2.50 postage & handling)

Ask for: "Choosing a Science Program for the Elementary School"

Write to: Council for Basic Education
725 15th St., N.W.
Washington, DC 20005

Teaching Sheets

The Massachusetts Audubon Society distributes teaching sheets on many topics of scientific interest for 10¢ a copy. Some of the sheets are one-sided, some two, but all are full of useful information and ideas. Categories covered include: Animals (How Animals Winter), Earth (Rocks and Minerals identification sheet), Flowers, Insects, and more. A complete list is available for free.

Send: a postcard

Ask for: "Teaching Sheets Guide"

Write to: Massachusetts Audubon Society
Educational Resources
South Great Road
Lincoln, MA 01773

Our Planet Earth

The World Federalist Association wants there to be a planet in every classroom. To fulfil this aim they are offering a poster of the NASA image of Earth seen from space, a powerful reminder of the beauty, fragility, and unity of our planet. This poster is not only an attractive classroom decoration, it is also a wonderful way to talk about our role in the universe.

Send: $4.00

Ask for: "An Earth Poster"

Write to: Kit Pineau or Willa Bernstein
World Federalist Association
777 U.N. Plaza
New York, NY 10017

Science Books Catalog

Dover Publications was a pioneer company in the field of science paperbacks, and in its 64-page catalog, it offers over 300 reasonably priced books covering subjects such as astronomy, physics, mathematics, chemistry, engineering, technology, geology, biology, and popular science.

Send: a postcard

Ask for: science catalog

Write to: Dover Publications, Inc.
31 E. 2nd St.
Mineola, NY 11501

Action Science Experiments

An innovative kit of 23 safe, motivational experiments for 3rd- to 6th-graders, each of which can be completed in 30 to 40 minutes. Using simple equipment commonly found at home and in school, children can try their hand at such terrific experiments as constructing a safety-pin telegraph.

Send: $2.95 (plus $1.00 postage & handling)

Ask for: "Action Science Experiments"

Write to: Teachers Exchange of San Francisco
28 Dawnview
San Francisco, CA 94131

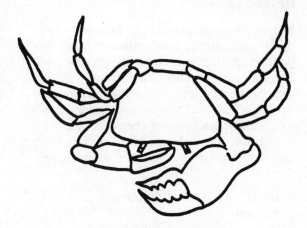

Land Hermit Crab Poster

Printed on both sides, this beautifully illustrated, informative 21-cm.-by-27-cm. poster is perfect for the bulletin board or display. Students will learn where a hermit crab lives, what he eats, and how he moves. Hermit crab activities are listed on the opposite side.

Send: $2.00 (plus $2.00 postage & handling)

Ask for: Land Hermit Crab poster

Write to: National Science Teachers Association
1742 Connecticut Ave., N.W.
Washington, DC 20009

Alchemy and Other Practical Sciences

Recent chemical discoveries and their practical applications are explored and explained in this collection of reprints from *The Science Teacher*. The articles explain the history of chemistry, delve into some of the basic building blocks, and include laboratory activities to make chemical theory familiar and bring students up to date with the excitement of current chemical research.

Send: $3.00 (plus $2.00 postage & handling)

Ask for: #PB-11 "From Alchemy to Accelerators"

Write to: National Science Teachers Association
Publications Dept. PL
1742 Connecticut Avenue, NW
Washington, DC 20009-1171

Science and Children Posters

The National Science Teachers Association offers some wonderful double-sided, full-color posters which are not only colorful and attractive, but also explain some simple science topics to children. They are 44 × 54 cm large and will liven up any classroom. Topics are: Extinction I, Extinction III, Dandelions, Marine Hitchhikers, Time, Insects, Bicycles, and Volcanos. Order each by name.

Send: $2.00 each (plus $2.00 postage and handling)

Ask for: poster desired

Write to: National Science Teachers Association
Publications Dept. PL
1742 Connecticut Avenue, NW
Washington, DC 20009-1171

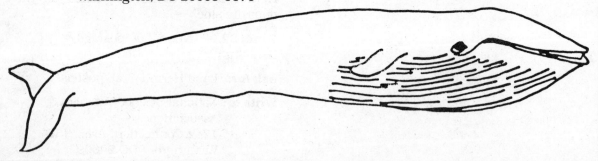

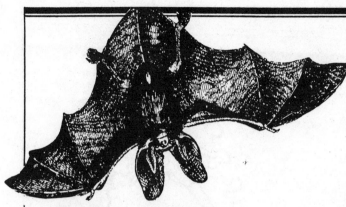

Audubon on Television

The Audubon Society has documentaries in production all around the world. They are currently filming specials on ancient forests, wolves, climate change, beaches and coastal pollution, dolphins and the ocean ecosystem, wildfire, tropical forests, overgrazing of public lands, and the Arctic National Wildlife Refuge. Be the first in your school to know when these films are coming out and what's next for the Audubon film crews. "The Audubon TV News Bulletin" will come to you free four times a year just for the asking.

Send: a postcard

Ask for: "The Audubon Television News Bulletin"

Write to: National Audubon Society
Television Department
801 Pennsylvania Avenue, SE
Washington, DC 20003

Color a Guppy

There are 41 different species of tropical fish, including the guppy, African knifefish, angelfish, piranha, and many others, as well as 26 species of marine plants, illustrated in this 8¼"-by-11" coloring book. Captions accompany each drawing.

Send: $2.50 (plus $2.50 postage & handling)

Ask for: "Tropical Fish Coloring Book"

Write to: Dover Publications, Inc.
31 E. 2nd St.
Mineola, NY 11501

Reforming Science Education

What is important for students to know in science? How should classwork be structured? What are the best teaching methods? The Council for Basic Education reevaluates the most effective and stimulating ways to present science to students.

Send: $2.00 (plus $2.50 postage & handling)

Ask for: "Reforming Science Education: The Search for a New Vision"

Write to: Council for Basic Education
725 15th St., N.W.
Washington, DC 20005

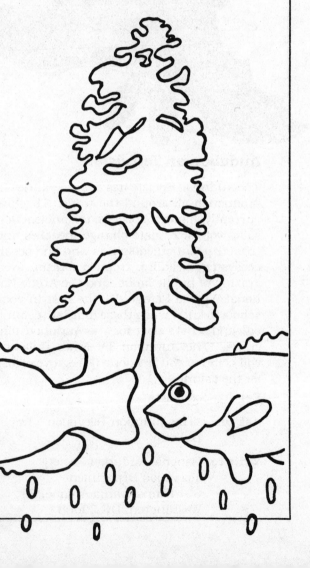

Entertaining Science Experiments

There is no better way to learn science than to actually experiment. Using everyday objects and supplies that can be found around any house or classroom, the 100 simple experiments in this book will amuse, astonish, entertain, and, most importantly, teach, your students the basic principles of science.

Send: $2.50 (plus $2.50 postage & handling)

Ask for: "Entertaining Science Experiments and Everyday Objects"

Write to: Dover Publications, Inc.
31 East 2nd Street
Mineola, NY 11501

Neighbors in the Solar System

Students love studying the solar system. It can spark their imaginations as they wonder about space travel and what life would be like on other planets. The Consumer Information Center offers an 8-page booklet with color photos and descriptions of the planets as well as information on spacecraft visits.

Send: $1.00

Ask for: 149W "Look at the Planets"

Write to: Consumer Information Catalog
P.O. Box 100
Pueblo, CO 81002

Windows on Wildlife

The New York Zoological Society publishes a series of six "Windows on Wildlife" booklets suitable for children aged nine through 12. Each of the six—"Grasslands," "Endangered Species," "Rain Forests," "Deciduous Forests," "Wetlands," and "Deserts"—is printed in two colors, is amply illustrated, and contains a glossary and bibliography for students and teachers. This series can form the nucleus of a six-part curriculum on wild animals and their natural habitats.

Send: $1.80 each

Ask for: desired title

Write to: Education Department
New York Zoological Society
Bronx Zoo
Bronx, NY 10460

Solar Fact Sheet

Solar energy is heat and light that comes from the sun. Thousands of years ago some people used this energy to heat their homes. Today, solar energy is again helping to heat buildings.

This five-page fact sheet printed by the Conservation and Renewable Energy Inquiry and Referral Service explains, in elementary language, the whys and hows of solar energy. Diagrams help describe the difference between passive and active collectors and also illustrate various types of heating systems. At the end, 10 questions test your knowledge. An easy way to learn the basics of solar energy.

Send: a postcard

Ask for: "Solar Fact Sheet"

Write to: Conservation and Renewable
Energy Inquiry and Referral
Service
P.O. Box 8900
Silver Spring, MD 20850

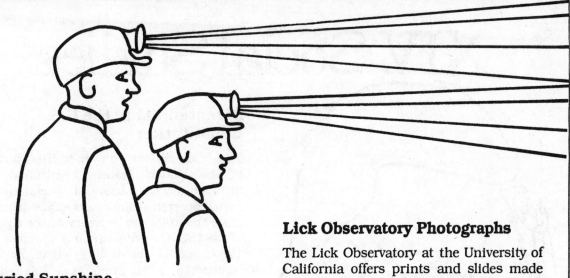

Buried Sunshine

This 16-page, two-color booklet titled "The Power from Coal" describes the beginnings, history, production, and uses of bituminous coal. A teacher's guide and student quizzes are included. Suitable for grades one through six.

Send: a postcard

Ask for: "The Power from Coal"

Write to: American Coal Foundation
1130 17th St., N.W.
Suite 220
Washington, DC 20036

Lick Observatory Photographs

The Lick Observatory at the University of California offers prints and slides made from astronomical photographs taken with its telescopes. The photographs are available in three standard formats: 35-mm. slides in 2″-by-2″ cardboard mounts, 8″-by-10″ glossy prints, and 14″-by-17″ glossy paper, dried-matte prints. The catalog shows a photograph of every print or slide available. California residents must add 6.5% tax.

Send: 50¢

Ask for: astronomical photographs catalog

Write to: Lick Observatory OP
University of California
Santa Cruz, CA 95064

XIV. Social Studies

Bicentennial of the U.S. Constitution

The Commission on the Bicentennial of the United States Constitution has included a wide variety of special educational programs among its plans to celebrate the 200th anniversary of the signing of the U.S. Constitution on September 17, 1787, and of the Bill of Rights on December 15, 1791. Students will delight in learning from free pocket-size copies of the Constitution. And bicentennial calendars—with day-by-day historical information on events that led to the signings—will also be available in 1987 and 1988. A perfect way to learn about the history of our unique legal system.

Send: a postcard

Ask for: pocket-size Constitution and free calendar

Write to: Commission on the Bicentennial of the United States Constitution
808 17th St., N.W.
Washington, DC 20006

Definitions of Racism

This 4-page pamphlet defines racism, describing the many obvious and subtle ways racism is manifest in American society. Complete with clear examples and explanations of the difference between racism and prejudice, this important publication provides vital eye-opening facts for kids and teachers. Set of 10 pamphlets.

Send: $2.00

Ask for: "Definitions of Racism"

Write to: Council on Interracial Books
CIBC Resource Center
1841 Broadway
New York, NY 10023

What Is a Dollar?

This pamphlet published by the Federal Reserve Bank of Boston takes a close look at the one dollar bill and at other types of U.S. currency. It explains how paper money was first created, what all those little numbers and codes really mean, and the value of the dollar as a medium of exchange. Students will also learn which president's portrait appears on which bill and other bits of trivia about U.S. currency.

What Is China All About?

China Books & Periodicals, the national importer of publications from China, offers a wide range of educational materials. Children's books, maps, posters, dictionaries, histories, novels, fairy tales, picture books, art prints, and note cards are only a few of the items offered. Write for their free catalog and welcome China into your classroom.

Send: a postcard

Ask for: catalog

Write to: China Books & Periodicals, Inc.
2929 24th St.
San Francisco, CA 94110

Send: a postcard

Ask for: "Dollar Points"

Write to: Publications Dept.
Federal Reserve Bank of Boston
600 Atlantic Ave. T-6
Boston, MA 02106

The Quakers

The Quakers were one of the first religious groups in America, and their story is both fascinating and unusual. From the mid-17th century to the present, this informative booklet traces the history of the Quakers in America. Details on modern-day Quaker institutions, beliefs, and life-style will acquaint children with an American way of life that may be very different from their own.

Send: $2.50 (plus $1.50 postage & handling)

Ask for: "The Quakers" (item no. 0904)

Write to: Publications Sales Program
Friends of the Pennsylvania
Historical and Museum
Commission
P.O. Box 1026
Harrisburg, PA 17108

United Nations Charter

This slim—57-page—edition contains the complete text of the Charter of the United Nations. Seeing the actual document is the best way to learn the purposes, principles, and structure of the United Nations. It can be used by teachers as a source for answering student questions or by the students themselves for research. A necessary item for any class in 20th-century history.

Send: $1.00

Ask for: "Charter of the United Nations"

Write to: U.N. Publications
D.C. 2
New York, NY 10017

Working Teenagers

The New York State United Teachers cooperated in the development of this 38-page resource guide to the rights of teenagers in the work force. It explains state laws governing wages, overtime, and health and welfare for teenagers. An excellent source for any guidance counselor, social studies teacher, or other concerned teacher or educator.

Send: a postcard

Ask for: "The Working Teenagers"

Write to: Paul Cole, Secretary-Treasurer
New York State AFLCIO
100 South Swan Street
Albany, NY 12210

A Visit to China and Japan

Take a pictorial journey to the Far East with University Prints. They offer two sets of 30 prints, $5\frac{1}{2}'' \times 8''$, which take you and your class to Asia and show you the many wonders there. Captioned illustrations include pictures of the major monuments and art forms that lend a distinctive flavor to each of these ancient cultures as it evolved through the centuries.

Send: $2.00 for each set (plus $1.00 postage & handling per order)

Ask for: "A Visit to China" or "A Visit to Japan"

Write to: The University Prints
21 East St., P.O. Box 485
Winchester, MA 01890

Yorktown

Relive the excitement of the Revolution- ary War period using the materials and activities included in this teacher's kit. Stu- dents can follow historical events and the progress of the Revolutionary War on a map provided for that purpose.

Send: $2.00

Ask for: "Yorktown"—teacher's kit

Write to: Education Department
Jamestown-Yorktown
Foundation
Drawer JF
Williamsburg, VA 23187

Building a History Curriculum

Drawing on their pool of respected historians and master classroom teachers from elementary and secondary levels, the Bradley Commission developed "Building a History Curriculum: Guidelines for Teaching History in Schools." This is a must-have for any history teacher. And now they have released a special reprint package of a six-part series which appeared in *History Matters!* which elaborates on the meaning of the themes beyond the introduction given in the "Guidelines."

Send: $1.00 and a self-addressed, stamped, #10 envelope for the reprint, and $3.00 for the guidelines

Ask for: "Building a History Curriculum: Guidelines for Teaching History in Schools" or "Vital Themes and Narratives"

Write to: The Bradley Commission Office
26915 Westwood Rd.
Suite A-2
Westlake, OH 44145

Expanding Horizons

"Expanding Horizons" is a 28-page report of a 1988 Bread Loaf Conference on Teacher Education and the Liberal Arts College. The Conference generated a wealth of ideas for integrating history and literature into the elementary curriculum, and they are all here, ready for you to use in your classroom.

Send: a postcard

Ask for: "Expanding Horizons: Creating Models for the Teaching of History and Literature at the Elementary School Level"

Write to: The Bradley Commission Office
26915 Westwood Rd.
Suite A-2
Westlake, OH 44145

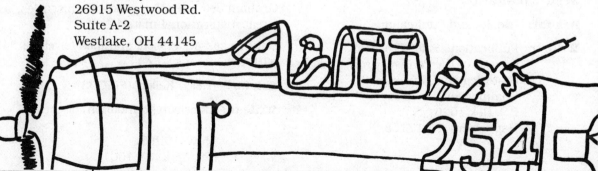

Historic Pennsylvania

The Pennsylvania Historical and Museum Commission publishes a number of fascinating books and pamphlets covering every aspect of Pennsylvania's history. Its list of books and publications is categorized by subject; some of the areas covered are the tercentenary, native Americans, the fight for independence, industry and work, culture and art, historical preservation, and Pennsylvania at war. A valuable resource for any teacher interested in teaching about our roots.

Send: a postcard

Ask for: "Books and Publications"

Write to: Publications Sales Program
Friends of the Pennsylvania
Historical and Museum
Commission
P.O. Box 1026
Harrisburg, PA 17108

Biography of Helen Keller

This 8-page pamphlet published by the American Foundation for the Blind describes the life of this extraordinary writer, who spent her adulthood working to help those less fortunate than herself. The pamphlet is filled with photographs of Keller with Charlie Chaplin, Alexander Graham Bell, and other goodwill emissaries. Great inspirational material.

Send: a self-addressed, stamped envelope with two stamps

Ask for: "Helen Keller" (FISO33)

Write to: American Foundation for the
Blind
15 W. 16th St.
New York, NY 10011

Grass Roots Preservation

Teach your students to preserve their history! The Champaign County Historical Museum of Champaign, Illinois, publishes a 24-page booklet that describes ways local historical organizations and school personnel can work together to develop preservation-related projects to supplement the social studies curriculum. The booklet is filled with photographs and a resource list is included.

Send: $2.00 and a self-addressed, stamped 5″ × 7″ envelope

Ask for: "Grass Roots Preservation"

Write to: Champaign County Historical Museum
709 W. University Ave.
Champaign, IL
61820

Turkish Delights

Topkapi Palace in Istanbul, Homer's Troy on the Aegean, Ataturk's Mausoleum in Ankara, and the breathtaking landscapes of the Black Sea Coast are just a few examples of this magical Mideastern country. The Turkish Embassy offers four brochures illustrating in full color other highlights.

Send: a postcard

Ask for: brochures on Turkey

Write to: Turkish Embassy
Office of the Tourism and
Information Counselor
821 United Nations Plaza
New York, NY 10017

From Geography to Politics

Numerous inexpensive publications on everything from different countries and people to governments and historical personalities are to be found among the multitude of educational books and pamphlets published by Troll Associates. Teachers will find numerous popular materials to supplement any social studies topic—indeed, just about any topic at all.

Send: request on school letterhead

Ask for: elementary paperback catalog

Write to: Troll Associates
100 Corporate Dr.
Mahwah, NJ 07430

History Through the Ages

This paper summarizes the suggestions offered by American historians from the 1800s to the present concerning the importance of studying history in public schools, what should be included, and how it should be taught. The authors use the results of past inquiries to shape new suggestions about teaching in the elementary grades. They conclude that history education is not only greatly affected by our society, but greatly affects it as well.

Send: $4.50

Ask for: "History in the Elementary
School Classroom" (Elementary
Subjects Center Series No. 2)

Write to: IRT Publications
Michigan State University
252 Erickson Hall
East Lansing, MI 48824-1034

My State and My Country

Millikin Publishing Company has two reproducible workbooks for intermediate social studies which are quite valuable. "Learning About My State" and "Learning About the USA" are full of independent and enrichment projects in the form of games, puzzles, and open-ended activities which familiarize students with their state capital, state government, resources, climate, and the U.S. regions.

Send: $4.95 each

Ask for: "Learning About My State" or
"Learning About the USA"

Write to: Milliken Publishing Company
1100 Research Blvd.
P.O. Box 21579
St. Louis, MO 63132-0579

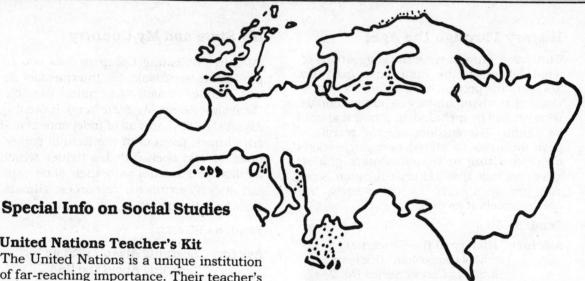

Special Info on Social Studies

United Nations Teacher's Kit
The United Nations is a unique institution of far-reaching importance. Their teacher's kit is of exceptional value, as it contains not only information on the workings of the UN itself, but also supplies details on how additional educational materials on many topical issues and world concerns can be obtained from various agencies and programs of the UN.

Send: a postcard

Ask for: Teacher's Kit

Write to: United Nations Public Inquiries
Unit
Room GA-57
United Nations
New York, NY 10017

The Heart of Europe

The Austrian Press and Information Service will provide you with a full-color guide to the Republic of Austria. Besides the usual statistical data, the brochure explains Austria's economic system, culture, and government. A brief history, map, and many photographs are included.

Send: a postcard

Ask for: "Austria at the Heart of Europe"

Write to: Austrian Press and Information
Service
31 E. 69th St.
New York, NY 10021

Teaching Taxes

The IRS provides high schools with a modular package of tax-education material including nine 15-minute videos, computer software that "walks" students through completion on tax forms, and detailed lesson plans with transparencies and duplicating masters. An invaluable resource for any social studies, history, civics, government, or economics teacher.

Call: 1-800-424-6081 (Ask for Educational Department)

Ask for: Form 1742

The American Revolution and the Civil War

The University Prints has sets of artistic depictions of the notable people and stirring events of two critical periods in the development of America. Each set of twenty captioned prints, $5^1/_2'' \times 8''$ in size, includes paintings and sculpture that capture the spirit of each age. An excellent way to combine an understanding of history with an appreciation of art.

Send: $1.50 each set (plus $1.00 postage & handling per order)

Ask for: "The American Revolution" or "The Civil War"

Write to: The University Prints
21 East St., P.O. Box 485
Winchester, MA 01890

A Visit to Ancient Egypt

Jump back to the age of Cleopatra, King Tut, and the Egyptian pyramids with this set of 66 prints. The colorful pictures illustrate the well-known people and sites of the era, as well as scenes depicting religion, art, crafts, and day-to-day life-styles of ancient Egyptians.

Send: $4.00 (plus $1.00 postage & handling)

Ask for: "A Visit to Ancient Egypt"

Write to: The University Prints
21 East St.
P.O. Box 485
Winchester, MA 01890

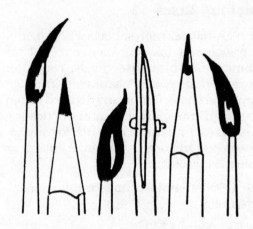

Napoleonic Uniforms

Learn while you color. This wonderful coloring book contains 45 full-page, ready-to-be-colored illustrations of Napoleonic Wars combatants. Captions beneath each picture provide identifications as to country and rank. A colorful bit of history just got more colorful.

Send: $2.50 (plus $2.50 postage & handling)

Ask for: "Uniforms of the Napoleonic Wars Coloring Book"

Write to: Dover Publications, Inc.
31 East 2nd Street
Mineola, NY 11501

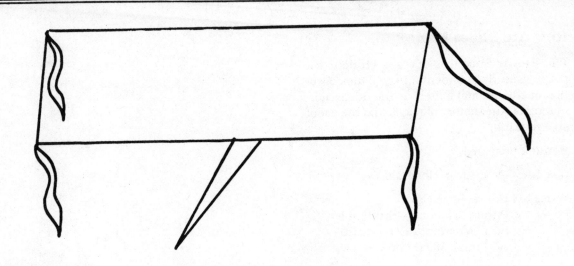

Making Money

Where does money actually come from? The bills themselves, we mean. The Department of the Treasury will send you a free brochure entitled "The Money Factory" which not only gives a brief history of the Bureau of Engraving and Printing, but also goes through the bill-making process step by step. Full of interesting pictures and trivia about the way money is made, this brochure can help a teacher explain and demonstrate a fascinating bit of Americana.

Send: a postcard

Ask for: "The Money Factory"

Write to: Public Affairs Department
Department of the Treasury
Bureau of Engraving and
Printing
Washington, D.C. 20228

How Are Shoes Made?

The Brown Shoe Co. offers a student kit titled "A Study of Shoemaking." This collection of educational materials includes information on the history of shoes and the art of shoemaking.

Send: a postcard

Ask for: "A Study in Shoemaking"

Write to: Brown Shoe Co.
Public Relations—Student Kit
8400 Maryland, P.O. Box 29
St. Louis, MO 63166

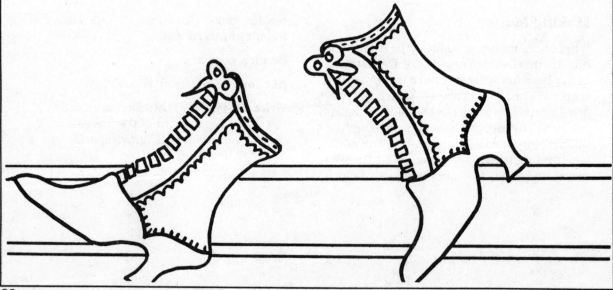

The FBI on the FBI

How many fingerprints does the FBI have on file? How does a criminal make it to the Ten Most Wanted list? What steps does the FBI take to counter terrorism? These and other questions on structure, jurisdiction, and methods of criminal investigation are answered in "FBI Facts and History," a new booklet being offered by the FBI itself. This booklet touches on many such questions and gives a bit of FBI history as well.

Send: a postcard

Ask for: "FBI Facts and History"

Write to: Publications
FBI Headquarters Rm. 6236
U.S. Dept. of Justice
Washington, DC 20535

How Money and Stamps Are Made

The Bureau of Engraving and Printing is the world's largest securities manufacturing establishment. It designs, engraves, and prints U.S. paper currency; Treasury bonds, bills, notes, and certificates of indebtedness; U.S. postage and revenue stamps; and over 800 miscellaneous items for various departments and agencies in the federal government. The operations of the bureau, including an examination of how currency and postage stamps are made, are offered in their free flier.

Send: a postcard

Ask for: "Production of Government Securities"

Write to: Public Affairs Dept.
Bureau of Engraving and Printing
14th and C St., S.W.
Washington, DC 20228

Earthquakes and Other Natural Disasters

Earthquakes can be very scary; especially to very little people. The "BIG BIRD Get Ready for Earthquakes" kit has been put together by the Children's Television Workshop (CTW) and the Federal Emergency Management Agency to help teach children about earthquakes, what to expect, and how to react if you are in one. The kit contains a booklet of tips in English and Spanish, a board game, and an audiotape with a lively song by Sesame Street regulars. A similar kit on hurricanes is also available, and other titles are planned.

Send: $2.25

Ask for: "BIG BIRD Get Ready for Earthquakes"

Write to: CTW
Dept. NH (L90)
One Lincoln Plaza
New York, NY
10023

Peace, War, and the Nuclear Threat

Some children start playing war games at a very early age—for example, learning to hit one another to solve problems. The National Association for the Education of Young Children believes in educating young children about the worldwide threat of war and nuclear arms. Toward that end, this book is designed to help adults instill in children a desire to seek peaceful solutions to problems.

Send: $3.00

Ask for: "Helping Young Children Understand Peace, War, and the Nuclear Threat" (NAEYC #321)

Write to: National Association for the Education of Young Children
1834 Connecticut Ave., N.W.
Washington, DC 20009

Historic Leaflets

Pennsylvania, the seat of liberty. Receive 41 free leaflets that tell you all about historic Pennsylvania. Topics include: biographies of James Buchanan and Chief Cornplanter, various historic battles and political events, the Liberty Bell, archeology, and much more. Filled with eye-catching pictures and intriguing information, these leaflets could be the basis of student papers, or used as handouts to supplement textbook reading.

Send: $4.00 (plus $1.00 postage & handling)

Ask for: "Pennsylvania Historic Leaflets" (Item no. 1501)

Write to: Publication Sales Program
Friends of the Pennsylvania
Historical and Museum
Commission
P.O. Box 1026
Harrisburg, PA 17108

XV. Special Children

Develop Reading Skills

Sometimes children with slight learning disabilities fall even further behind because reading is so taxing that it simply isn't worth the effort. High Noon books are the key to stopping this downward spiral. Specially designed high interest/low readability books have great (and simple) plots, large type, and attractive covers that could draw even the most reluctant reader. They also have games, audiocassette books, and Spanish editions.

Send: a postcard

Ask for: a catalog

Write to: High Noon Books
20 Commercial Boulevard
Novato, CA 94949-6191

Early Warning Signs

Some children are born with physical or mental conditions—or they may acquire disorders that handicap normal growth and development. Fortunately, many of these conditions can be corrected if parents and teachers recognize the problem early and seek help. A pamphlet published by The National Easter Seal Society lists some of the early warning signs and some of the more common indications that a problem may exist. They also list people and organizations that can help.

Send: 35¢ for 3

Ask for: "Are You Listening to What Your Child May Not Be Saying?"

Write to: The National Easter Seal Society
70 E. Lake St.
Chicago, IL 60601

Stuttering Words

The Speech Foundation of America has published an authoritative glossary of the meanings of the words and terms used or associated with the field of stuttering, speech pathology, and its treatment. A unique and educational guide.

Send: 50¢ (plus $1.00 postage & handling)

Ask for: "Stuttering Words, Publication No. 2"

Write to: Speech Foundation of America
P.O. Box 11749
Memphis, TN 38111

For the Learning Disabled

The 13th edition of the "Directory of Facilities and Services for Learning Disabled" lists hundreds of organizations in the U.S. and Canada of help to the parents and teachers of learning-disabled students. The name, address, telephone number, and information on staff is included for each facility listed.

Send: $3.00

Ask for: "Directory of Facilities and Services for Learning Disabled"

Write to: Academic Therapy Publications
20 Commercial Blvd.
Novato, CA 94949

Helping the Gifted Child

"He is the kind of child a teacher dreams of having once in a lifetime. But now that we have him, we don't know what to do with him." How many teachers have uttered the same words as this teacher of a fifth-grader who was blessed with an IQ of 169? More often than not, to be a gifted child in a school is to be a handicapped child, but Drs. James Gallagher and Patricia Weiss are trying to remedy the problem. In their booklet, these educators explain what giftedness means and detail the emerging opportunites for the education of the gifted and specially talented student.

Send: $2.00 (plus $2.50 postage & handling)

Ask for: "The Education of Gifted and Talented Students"

Write to: Council for Basic Education
725 15th St., N.W.
Washington, DC 20005

When You Have a Visually Handicapped Child in Your Classroom

This 28-page handbook lists practical suggestions for the teacher who has a visually handicapped student in the regular classroom. It includes advice about attitudes, mobility, materials, resources, personnel, and information about special devices. A bibliography and organizations list is also included.

Send: a self-addressed, stamped envelope with 3 stamps

Ask for: "When You Have a Visually Handicapped Child in Your Classroom" (FEL057)

Write to: American Foundation for the Blind
15 W. 16th St.
New York, NY 10011

Disabling Myths About Disability

Without realizing it, we often perpetuate myths about disability, and these habitual ways of thinking can hinder full human expression. Teachers especially should examine their attitudes and work to counteract any that might be harmful to students. In this pamphlet published by the National Easter Seal Society, Bernice A. Wright, professor of psychology at the University of Kansas, examines the myths and the mischief they create.

Send: $1.20

Ask for: "Disabling Myths About Disability"

Write to: The National Easter Seal Society
70 E. Lake St.
Chicago, IL 60624

XVI. Sports, Games, and Hobbies

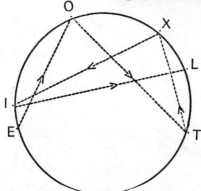

Beginner's Compass Game

The Beginner's Compass Game is an exciting way to learn proper compass usage. The game is easy to set up and requires little space or equipment. Plans for 90 different games are included.

Send: $1.50

Ask for: Beginner's Compass Game

Write to: Orienteering Services, U.S.A.
P.O. Box 1604
Binghamton, NY 13902

Roller Skates

In the past few years, roller skating has become one of the most popular sports in America. The Chicago Roller Skate Co. offers two booklets that include information on skating skills and safety. Both are illustrated and easy to read.

Send: 50¢ plus self-addressed, stamped envelope

Ask for: "How to Roller Skate" and "Skating Skills"

Write to: Chicago Roller Skate Co.
4245 W. Lake St.
Chicago, IL 60624

Unlimited Orienteering

Orienteering began in Sweden in the early 1900s as a military exercise. Today these "forest drills" are among the most popular recreational activities in the country, and their appeal is becoming known around the world. Not only is orienteering good for the body, it's also good for the mind—teaching reasoning and logic skills. Orienteering Unlimited is an organization solely devoted to the propagation of this sport. Their catalog has orienteering games, supplies, videotapes, books, bumper stickers, and so on—everything you could ever need to start your own orienteering program.

Send: a postcard

Ask for: A catalog

Write to: Orienteering Unlimited, Inc.
Jan Ridge Road
Somers, NY 10589

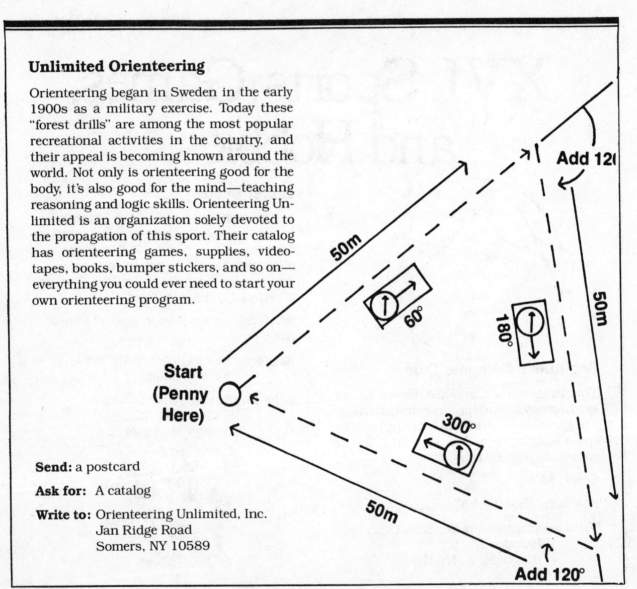

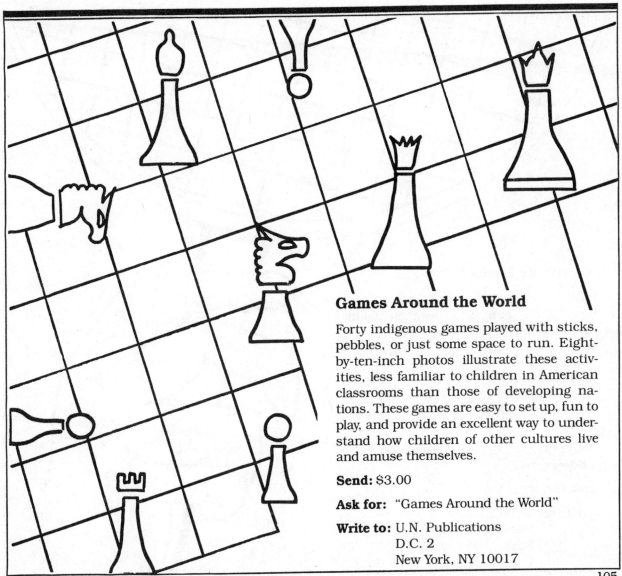

Games Around the World

Forty indigenous games played with sticks, pebbles, or just some space to run. Eight-by-ten-inch photos illustrate these activities, less familiar to children in American classrooms than those of developing nations. These games are easy to set up, fun to play, and provide an excellent way to understand how children of other cultures live and amuse themselves.

Send: $3.00

Ask for: "Games Around the World"

Write to: U.N. Publications
D.C. 2
New York, NY 10017

Everyone Loves a Pen Pal

Having pen pals can be great fun for children. They can write to their far-away friends about all the things they like to do: play tennis, draw, skateboard—whatever! Children interested in corresponding with pen pals can "meet" boys and girls ages 7–17. Each child receives three names and addresses of children of approximately the same age.

Send: $2.00 (plus name, complete address, and age)

Ask for: "Pen Pals"

Write to: Jolie Coins
P.O. Box 399
Roslyn Heights, NY 11577

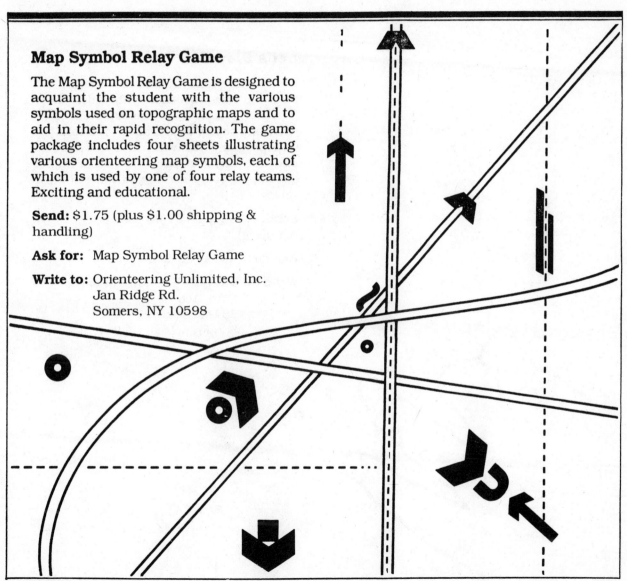

Map Symbol Relay Game

The Map Symbol Relay Game is designed to acquaint the student with the various symbols used on topographic maps and to aid in their rapid recognition. The game package includes four sheets illustrating various orienteering map symbols, each of which is used by one of four relay teams. Exciting and educational.

Send: $1.75 (plus $1.00 shipping & handling)

Ask for: Map Symbol Relay Game

Write to: Orienteering Unlimited, Inc.
Jan Ridge Rd.
Somers, NY 10598

Let's Play Ball

Basketball, volleyball, and kickball are three all-time favorites with kids. "Let's Play Ball," designed by an experienced elementary school P.E. teacher, is a step-by-step program that will aid in creating an effective physical education program for developing coordination and skills in these sports.

Send: $2.95 (plus $1.00 postage & handling)

Ask for: "Let's Play Ball"

Write to: Teachers Exchange of San Francisco
28 Dawnview
San Francisco, CA 94131

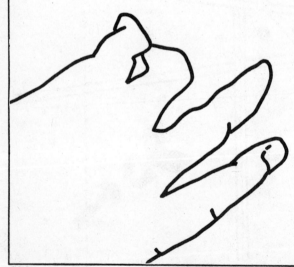

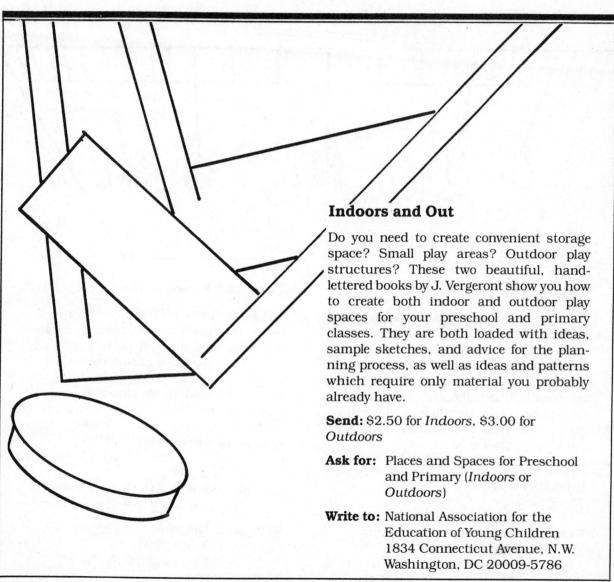

Indoors and Out

Do you need to create convenient storage space? Small play areas? Outdoor play structures? These two beautiful, hand-lettered books by J. Vergeront show you how to create both indoor and outdoor play spaces for your preschool and primary classes. They are both loaded with ideas, sample sketches, and advice for the planning process, as well as ideas and patterns which require only material you probably already have.

Send: $2.50 for *Indoors*, $3.00 for *Outdoors*

Ask for: Places and Spaces for Preschool and Primary (*Indoors* or *Outdoors*)

Write to: National Association for the Education of Young Children 1834 Connecticut Avenue, N.W. Washington, DC 20009-5786

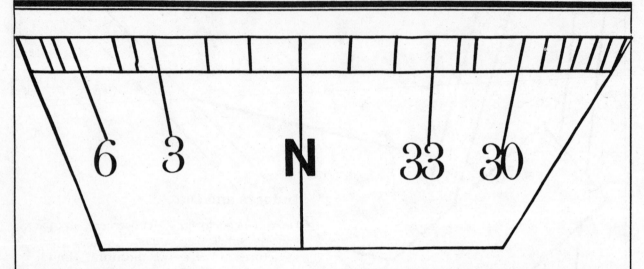

Compass Game

The Compass Game (feet or Metric) is designed to assist teachers in imparting the basic compass skills of setting bearings and pacing to specific locations. The game is fun and competitive and provides compass training without elaborate preparation. The 20 separate trails, each having three directions of travel, are automatically established by setting out a row of stakes.

Send: $1.75 (plus $1.00 postage and handling per order)

Ask for: Compass Game

Write to: Orienteering Unlimited, Inc.
Jan Ridge Rd.
Somers, NY 10598

Coin and Paper Money Collecting

Collecting coins and/or paper money is a hobby that many people enjoy their whole lives. Get your students off to a good start with 14 different coins/notes from Jolie Coins. They will send samples from such countries as Indonesia, Brazil, Cyprus, Korea, Israel, or Finland. These could also be used by a teacher to show how money differs around the world.

Send: $2.00

Ask for: "Start a Collection of Foreign Coins and Paper Money"

Write to: Jolie Coins
P.O. Box 339T
Roslyn Heights, NY 11577

The Importance of Play

An educator who plays with children may rediscover his or her own creative responses and the pleasure of moving expressively. Montessori educators believe that play and creative interaction are important parts of a child's education—play can be a significant way of expressing the joy of being oneself. Guidelines for encouraging the child to discover the dance from within are offered in a booklet published by the American Montessori Society.

Send: $1.00

Ask for: X108 "Play Behaviors of Young Children"

Write to: American Montessori Society
150 Fifth Ave.
New York, NY 10011

Benjamin Franklin Stamp Clubs

The Benjamin Franklin Stamp Club Program was founded in 1974 to teach the educational and recreational values of stamp collecting to grade school students. Teachers receive an extensive Teacher's Guide, an Activity Guide, a brochure called "Introduction to Stamp Collecting," the newsletters "Stamp Fun" and "Leader Feature," and special resources such as coloring books, a Stamposaurus puzzle, posters, the "Treasury of Stamps Album," and many others.

Send: a postcard

Ask for: "Benjamin Franklin Stamp Club Information"

Write to: Your local post office

Stamps on Film

The United States Postal Service offers seven free films about stamp collecting. From the seven-minute "America the Beautiful"—a colorful film that relates recent stamp design to the natural beauty and scenic wonders of America—to the fifty-minute "The Video Guide to Stamp Collecting," these films are perfect for new collectors and a treat for experienced collectors, too. Order the catalog to learn all about these seven films.

Send: a postcard

Ask for: "Catalog of Free Loan Films"

Write to: Philatelic Marketing Division
United States Postal Service
Washington, D.C. 20265-9994

Nature Stamps

Get Olympic stamps from Yemen. Fish stamps from the Soviet Union. Universal Publishing offers a set of 100 different over-sized foreign stamps, each depicting nature in its beauty and diversity. These stamps will provide either a wonderful starter kit or more fodder for the serious stamp enthusiast.

Send: $2.00

Ask for: "Nature Stamps"

Write to: Universal Publishing Co. of Port, Inc.
P.O. Box 226
Port Washington, NY 11050

Origami for Beginners

Origami is a wonderful hobby because it can be simple enough for a young child to learn and is complicated enough to keep a master challenged for years. "Paper Folding for Beginners" is an excellent introduction into the art of origami. Clear instructions, and over 275 illustrations, make creating sail boats, roosters, frogs that have legs that move, etc., a breeze.

Send: $2.50 (plus $2.50 postage & handling)

Ask for: "Paper Folding for Beginners"

Write to: Dover Publications, Inc.
31 East 2nd Street
Mineola, NY 11501

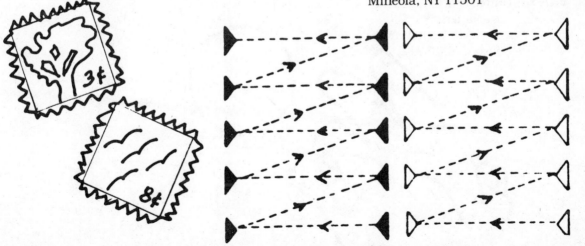

All About Handball

Do you need one good reason to add Handball to your Physical Education Program? Well, the U.S. Handball Association has twelve of them. Get their free brochure "Handball: Challenge, Fitness and Fun for a Lifetime" and learn all about handball and what the U.S.H.A. has to offer. You'll get quotes from famous people, an explanation of the various types of handball, and a list of resource material available from the U.S.H.A.

Send: a postcard

Ask for: "Handball: Challenge, Fitness and Fun for a Lifetime"

Write to: United States Handball Association
930 North Benton Avenue
Tucson, AZ 85711

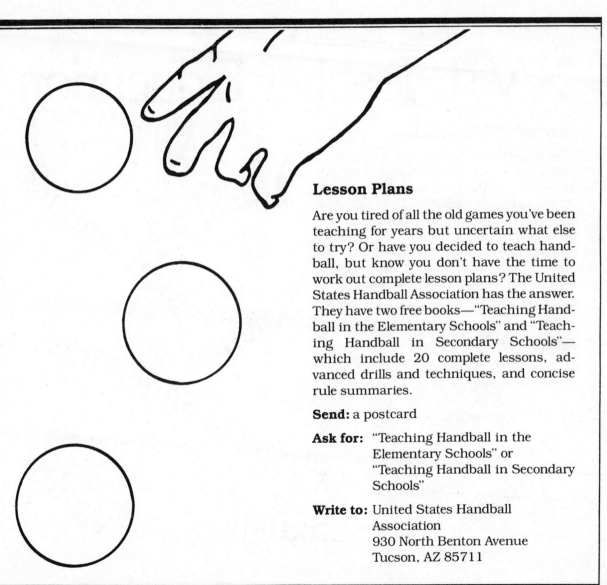

Lesson Plans

Are you tired of all the old games you've been teaching for years but uncertain what else to try? Or have you decided to teach handball, but know you don't have the time to work out complete lesson plans? The United States Handball Association has the answer. They have two free books—"Teaching Handball in the Elementary Schools" and "Teaching Handball in Secondary Schools"—which include 20 complete lessons, advanced drills and techniques, and concise rule summaries.

Send: a postcard

Ask for: "Teaching Handball in the Elementary Schools" or "Teaching Handball in Secondary Schools"

Write to: United States Handball Association
930 North Benton Avenue
Tucson, AZ 85711

XVII. Teacher Education

Curriculum Management

The conditions that make important differences in schools are the instructional leadership of the principal, definition of purpose, expectations of students, and time spent "on task." In his 26-page paper, Fenwick English describes the strenuous measures he feels are required to improve school curriculum. English is a former teacher, principal, and superintendent.

Send: $2.00 (plus $2.50 postage & handling)

Ask for: "Improving Curriculum Management in the Schools"

Write to: Council for Basic Education
725 15th St., N.W.
Washington, DC 20005

Art

Music

Mathematics

Science

Physical education

History

English

Health

What Works in School

Ever wonder how effective it is to have your students memorize the multiplication table? Does assigning a large amount of homework help the child? What is the best way to manage classroom time? The U.S. Department of Education offers an 86-page booklet filled research findings, comments, and resources on some of the questions most frequently asked by teachers.

Send: $3.00

Ask for: "What Works: Research About Teaching and Learning"

Write to: What Works
Pueblo, CO 81009

Teachers and A.A.

Alcoholics Anonymous, the reputable fellowship of men and women who believe that alcoholism is a disease that can be controlled, publishes a number of booklets of interest to educators. "A Brief Guide to Alcoholics Anonymous" defines the disease, explains the nature of the organization, and tells where to find more information. If you think you might have a problem, or suspect that one of your students might, this is a welcome and instructive pamphlet.

Send: 15¢

Ask for: P-42

Write to: A.A. World Services, Inc.
P.O. Box 459
Grand Central Station
New York, NY 10163

Burnout

Burnout is defined as physical, emotional, and attitudinal exhaustion. It may show up as low staff morale, frequent absenteeism, or high job turnover. Teachers are particularly prone to burnout; indeed, some fear that burnout has reached epidemic proportions. ERIC offers a fact sheet that discusses the ailment and cites possible personal and institutional remedies.

Send: a postcard

Ask for: Fact Sheet Number 3

Write to: ERIC Clearinghouse on
Urban Education
Box 40
Teachers College
Columbia University
New York, NY 10027

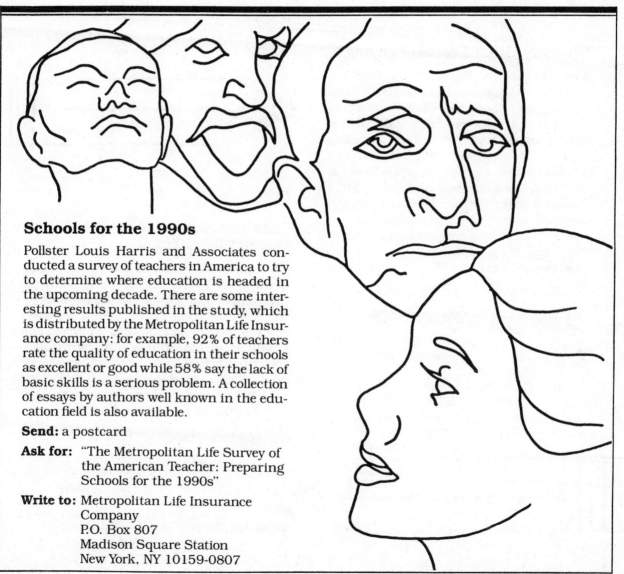

Schools for the 1990s

Pollster Louis Harris and Associates conducted a survey of teachers in America to try to determine where education is headed in the upcoming decade. There are some interesting results published in the study, which is distributed by the Metropolitan Life Insurance company: for example, 92% of teachers rate the quality of education in their schools as excellent or good while 58% say the lack of basic skills is a serious problem. A collection of essays by authors well known in the education field is also available.

Send: a postcard

Ask for: "The Metropolitan Life Survey of the American Teacher: Preparing Schools for the 1990s"

Write to: Metropolitan Life Insurance Company
P.O. Box 807
Madison Square Station
New York, NY 10159-0807

What Are Other Teachers Saying?

The Institute for Research on Teaching publishes "Communication Quarterly," an informative bulletin that covers subjects of interest to today's teachers. The IRT is funded by a variety of sources, including the U.S. Department of Education and Michigan State University, and is based at the College of Education at Michigan State University. Recent articles have covered methods of motivating students, teaching science, and improving reading and writing skills. Important for any teacher who wants to keep up to date.

Send: a postcard

Ask for: sample of "Communication Quarterly"

Write to: Editor—"Communication Quarterly"
Institute for Research on Teaching—MSU
252 Erickson Hall
East Lansing, MI 48824-1034

Uses and Abuses of Standardized Tests

On the whole, reading readiness tests and the approach of which they are a part do more harm than good. It would be wiser to begin formal reading instruction, as some schools do, by attempting to teach all children the same things, without prejudging or predicting their success. These ideas and others are elaborated in a booklet written by George Weber, associate director for the Council for Basic Education.

Send: $2.00 (plus $2.50 postage & handling)

Ask for: "Uses and Abuses of Standardized Testing in the Schools"

Write to: Council for Basic Education
725 15th St., N.W.
Washington, DC 20005

Submit Your Paper to ERIC

The staff of ERIC, the Educational Resources Information Center, invites you to submit your document to their clearinghouse. If accepted, the document will become part of a permanent collection in microfiche and will be available in over 650 libraries and other facilities throughout the world. ERIC is interested in documents relevant to urban life and schooling; the education of urban minorities; the performance of urban children; the effects of urban experiences on children and adults; economic and ethnic discrimination, segregation, and integration; and many other areas. This brochure provides full information.

Send: a postcard

Ask for: "ERIC/CUE Invites You to Submit Your Documents to ERIC"

Write to: ERIC Clearinghouse on Urban Education
Box 40
Teachers College
Columbia University
New York, NY 10027

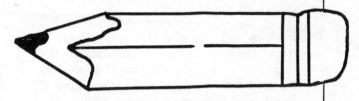

Racism in Our Language

Language is an integral part of any culture. It not only develops in conjunction with a society's historical, economic, and political evolution, but also reflects the society's attitudes and thinking. It not only expresses ideas and concepts, but actually shapes thoughts. If one accepts that our dominant white culture is racist, then one would expect our language to be racist as well. In this essay published by the Council on Interracial Books, the author describes the ways our language transmits racist concepts and outlines five lesson plans for detecting racist language and practicing nonracist language.

Send: $2.50

Ask for: "Racism in the English Language"

Write to: The Council on Interracial Books
CIBC Resource Center
1841 Broadway
New York, NY 10023

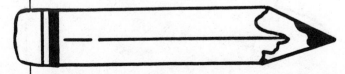

School Reform

In this important document, theory is translated into four practical recommendations for policy development in schools. Concise text by researchers Marshall S. Smith and Stewart C. Purkey provides an admirable model for school improvement.

Send: $2.00 (plus $2.50 postage & handling)

Ask for: "School Reform: The District Policy Implication of the Effective Schools Literature"

Write to: Council for Basic Education
725 15th St., N.W.
Washington, DC 20005

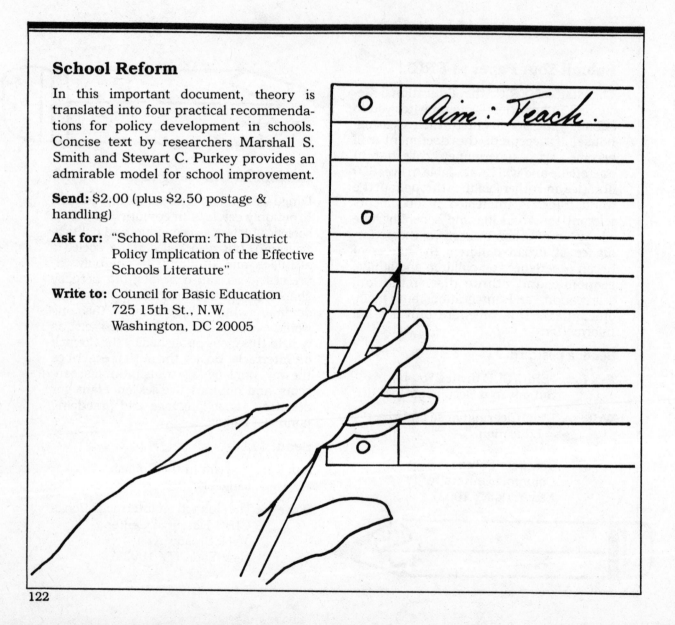

The Stepchild of American Education

Although in-service training ought to be a vitally important part of the preparation of teachers to meet their responsibilities, it has been called the stepchild of American education. The implication is unfortunate, not only because many teachers enter their profession inadequately prepared, or because declining enrollments mean that the schools will depend increasingly on "old" teachers who need "retreading." The fact is that good teachers develop their competence during the course of experience. Peter Greer, superintendent of schools in Portland, Maine, expounds on his views in this important 24-page paper.

Send: $2.00 (plus $2.50 postage & handling)

Ask for: "Education's Stepchild, In-service Training"

Write to: Council for Basic Education
725 15th St., N.W.
Washington, DC 20005

Academic Therapy

Diagnosing and teaching the learning-disabled child are often delicate and difficult even for the most experienced professionals. Academic Therapy Publications provides tests, methods of interpretation, software, special publications, and numerous other teaching aids to help facilitate the complex issues and teaching processes involved in working with learning-disabled children. Their catalog is an invaluable reference not only for specialists, but for teachers of all subjects.

Send: a postcard

Ask for: a catalog

Write to: Academic Therapy Publications
20 Commercial Blvd.
Novato, CA 94949

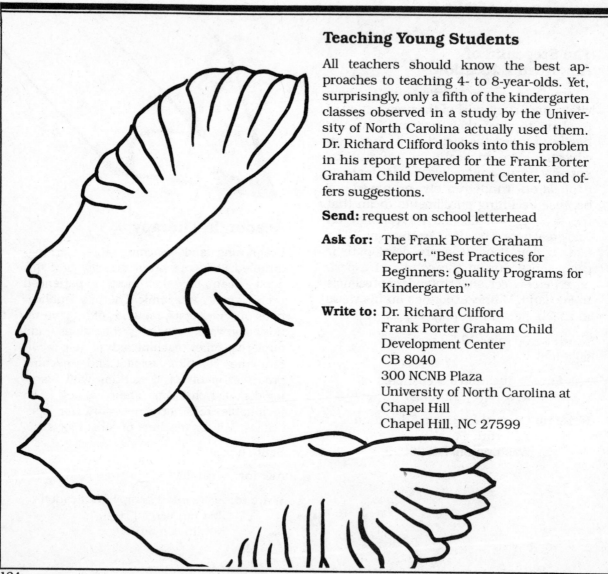

Teaching Young Students

All teachers should know the best approaches to teaching 4- to 8-year-olds. Yet, surprisingly, only a fifth of the kindergarten classes observed in a study by the University of North Carolina actually used them. Dr. Richard Clifford looks into this problem in his report prepared for the Frank Porter Graham Child Development Center, and offers suggestions.

Send: request on school letterhead

Ask for: The Frank Porter Graham Report, "Best Practices for Beginners: Quality Programs for Kindergarten"

Write to: Dr. Richard Clifford
Frank Porter Graham Child Development Center
CB 8040
300 NCNB Plaza
University of North Carolina at Chapel Hill
Chapel Hill, NC 27599

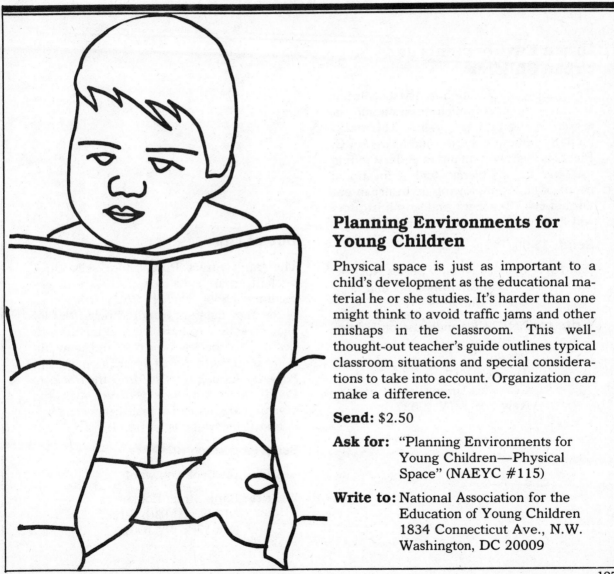

Planning Environments for Young Children

Physical space is just as important to a child's development as the educational material he or she studies. It's harder than one might think to avoid traffic jams and other mishaps in the classroom. This well-thought-out teacher's guide outlines typical classroom situations and special considerations to take into account. Organization *can* make a difference.

Send: $2.50

Ask for: "Planning Environments for Young Children—Physical Space" (NAEYC #115)

Write to: National Association for the Education of Young Children 1834 Connecticut Ave., N.W. Washington, DC 20009

Urban Environments and Urban Children

The quality of education in city schools has been the subject of much question and research in the past few years. This document by James Garbarino and Margaret C. Plantz is an important aid to understanding the unique problems and educational needs of children growing up in urban environments. Teachers and administrators will find this study enlightening.

Send: $2.00

Ask for: Urban Diversity Series No. 69: "Urban Environments and Urban Children"

Write to: ERIC Clearinghouse on Urban Education
Box 40
Teachers College
Columbia University
New York, NY 10027

Book Lists

The Bank Street Book Store sells three books that are extremely useful to the elementary-school teacher. *Children's Books of the Year* lists six hundred new titles for ages preschool to fourteen and includes titles of paperbacks, reprints, and new editions, along with a brief description of each. *Paperback Books for Children* and *Books to Read Aloud* are more general, spanning several years instead of just the present one. Each title is available for $4.00.

Send: $4.00 each title

Ask for: the book you want

Write to: Bank Street Bookstore
610 West 112th Street
New York, NY 10025

ou in house

out	pound
loud	shout
noun	scout
found	mountain
sound	fountain

Bilingual Education in the United States

With ever-increasing numbers of non-English-speaking children entering the U.S. school systems, bilingual education has become a serious question. This study provides background material and an interesting perspective, including past and present progress, problems, and possible solutions.

Send: $2.00

Ask for: "Urban Diversity Series No. 68: "Bilingual Education in the United States—A View from 1980"

Write to: ERIC Clearinghouse on Urban Education
Box 40
Teachers College
Columbia University
New York, NY 10027

Susan Osborn is a freelance writer and
part-time teacher.